THE
HISTORY
BOOK

First published in 2015 by
Miles Kelly Publishing Ltd
Harding's Barn, Bardfield End Green,
Thaxted, Essex, CM6 3PX, UK

Copyright © Miles Kelly Publishing Ltd 2015

This edition printed 2016

10 9 8 7 6 5 4 3 2

Publishing Director Belinda Gallagher
Creative Director Jo Cowan
Managing Editor Amanda Askew
Managing Designer Simon Lee

Senior Editor Claire Philip
Assistant Editors Amy Johnson, Lauren White
Designer Simon Lee
Proofreaders Carly Blake, Fran Bromage
Image Manager Liberty Newton
Production Elizabeth Collins, Caroline Kelly
Reprographics Stephan Davis,
Jennifer Cozens, Thom Allaway
Assets Lorraine King

ISBN 978-1-78209-842-3

Printed in China

British Library Cataloging-in-Publication Data
A catalog record for this book is available
from the British Library

Made with paper from a sustainable forest

www.mileskelly.net

THE
HISTORY
BOOK

Contributors

Simon Adams

Philip Steele

Stewart Ross

Richard Platt

Miles
KeLLY

Contents

History REVEALED

Go back in time and uncover a host of extreme events, ideas, and people that changed the course of history.

◀ The movie *Troy* (2004) tells the story of the Trojan War—the ancient Greeks believed a great war, lasting for ten years, was fought in the 1200s BC between the Greeks and the Trojans.

Living DEAD

The ancient Egyptians believed that a dead person's spirit needed a body to reach the afterlife—another stage of life, after death. To preserve the corpse, they developed the process of mummification.

▼ The mummy-makers washed the corpse before cutting it open to remove vital organs.

1 Body wash

In the first 15 days, the body was cleaned. It was taken to a tent, known as the Place of Purification, where it was washed with salty water, before being slit open and the insides removed. The brain was discarded, but the liver, lungs, intestines, and stomach were kept. The heart was left inside the body because the ancient Egyptians believed that it was needed to guide the person into the next life.

A HEARTY MEAL

The heart, as the core of a person's personality, was preserved within the mummified body. The ancient Egyptians believed that before a dead person could receive eternal life, the god Anubis had to weigh their heart on a balance against the Feather of Truth. If it proved heavier than the feather—a sign of a wicked life—the heart was devoured by the Swallowing Monster, which killed the person.

2 Bottled body bits

Vital organs such as the lungs, stomach, intestines, and liver were dried. Once they had been dried out in salt, the organs were stored in special stone or ceramic containers called canopic jars. These were sealed with lids shaped like the head of one of the four sons of the god Horus.

◄ The intestines were placed in the hawk-headed canopic jar. The hawk represented the god Qebehsenuef.

3 Drying out

To prevent the flesh from rotting over time, all the moisture needed to be removed. Mummy-makers stuffed the corpse with a special salt called natron, before placing it in a natron-filled bath for 40 days. The body became shriveled, hard, and blue-black in color.

◀ The corpse is covered in natron—up to 500 lb (225 kg)—to draw out all the moisture.

1 Head wrapped and Eye of Horus placed over the slit where the organs were removed

2 Body and limbs wrapped

3 Whole body wrapped

4 Bandaging complete

5 Enclosed in canvas sheet

4 Well wrapped

After the natron was removed, the dried-out (desiccated) corpse was oiled and given false eyes and a wig to make it appear more lifelike. Then a resin was poured over the corpse to set it hard and stop mold from growing. Finally, the body was stuffed with linen and even sawdust, then wrapped in 50 ft (15 m) of linen bandages over 15 prayer-filled days.

◀ The five-stage sequence of wrapping the body always started with the head. During the wrapping, lucky amulets were placed between the bandages to protect the person from harm in the afterlife.

5 Precious possessions

Finally the preserved body was placed inside a wooden case. As death was seen as a temporary break in life, mummies were buried with everyday items such as jewelry, clothing, shoes, musical instruments, and furniture. Pet cats and dogs were also mummified to keep their owners company in the afterlife.

◀ Expensive coffins were shaped like a person and decorated with spells. Bodily features such as eyes helped the person to transfer into the afterlife.

▶ This mummy was found after 4,000 years. Its features are still recognizable because of the preservation techniques of the ancient Egyptians.

Battle BEASTS

During early warfare, commanders used a variety of animals to gain an edge over their enemy. The most common was the horse—it carried cavalry, pulled chariots, and transported heavy loads. The camel, though slower, served well in desert campaigns. By far the most spectacular warrior animal was the mighty elephant, a living tank that trampled and terrorized its foes across Asia, North Africa, and Southern Europe.

▼ In 218 BC, the Carthaginian general Hannibal launched a surprise attack on his Roman enemies by leading an army, backed by war-trained elephants, across the Alps and into Italy. Hannibal won three great victories before he was forced to retire.

Anti-elephant

Ears flapping, trunk raised, tusks lancing... the awesome sight of a war elephant on the charge was enough to turn the legs of the bravest warrior to jelly. However, tactics were devised to halt the 30-mph (50-km/h) onslaught. The Romans learned to step aside at the last minute, Alexander the Great's men slashed at the beasts' hamstrings with axes, the Mongols catapulted rocks at them, and in more modern times the beasts were brought down by cannon fire.

Charge!

While several peoples of Central Asia were renowned for being able to shoot arrows accurately while on horseback, it was only with the invention of the stirrup in the 4th century AD that cavalry came into their own. Their grandest form was the mounted medieval knight. Although no longer armored, cavalry remained a vital element of warfare well into the 20th century.

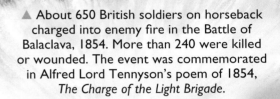

▲ About 650 British soldiers on horseback charged into enemy fire in the Battle of Balaclava, 1854. More than 240 were killed or wounded. The event was commemorated in Alfred Lord Tennyson's poem of 1854, *The Charge of the Light Brigade*.

▲ During World War I (1914–1918), dogs were not only used to deliver messages, but also to transport machine guns.

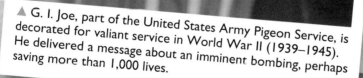

▲ G. I. Joe, part of the United States Army Pigeon Service, is decorated for valiant service in World War II (1939–1945). He delivered a message about an imminent bombing, perhaps saving more than 1,000 lives.

Woof and wing

Humans are slow and vulnerable message carriers. Before it was possible to send messages by radio, there was no better way of quickly delivering long-range information than tying it to the leg of a carrier pigeon; and no one could beat a messenger dog when it came to bounding over treacherous terrain.

THE U.S. NAVY ONCE TRAINED DOLPHINS TO SEEK OUT FROGMEN WHO WERE TRYING TO BREACH THE SECURITY AROUND SHIPS AND BASES.

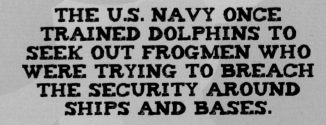

Camel corps

The Imperial Camel Corps (1916–1918) was manned by British, Indian, Australian, and New Zealand riders and served with distinction in the Middle East during World War I (1914–1918). The camel's ability to go for five days without water made it ideal for desert operations.

Extreme SIEGE

A medieval castle was an uncompromising symbol of the owner's power, might, and majesty, and if it fell, their importance and prestige tumbled with it. The masterbuilder's task, therefore, was to use every possible form of defense, from crenellations to moats, to make it as impregnable as possible. Outside, attackers devised whatever means they could to break through the stronghold.

KEY

Attack

Defense

Trebuchet The gravity-powered machine, while slow to operate, could hurl a 300-lb (140-kg) rock several hundred feet.

Archers A rain of arrows from castle-top defenders forced attackers back.

Wall The incredibly thick stone wall was built smooth-faced and splayed at the bottom to hinder attackers.

Crenellation Battlements that offered shelter for defenders.

Infantry As most castles were eventually starved into submission rather than taken by direct assault, the infantry had to remain alert to prevent outside supplies being taken in.

Mangonel The torsion-powered siege engine, like a gigantic catapult, used a metal spring or, more usually, twisted horsehair.

Hoarding A temporary wooden structure with a high viewpoint, from which defenders could fire arrows.

Boiling water Defenders poured it onto enemies as they climbed the walls.

Tower By the 14th century, the strongest towers were clustered around the castle's weakest point, the gate.

Machicolation An opening through which attackers were assaulted with arrows or bombarded with hot oil and stones.

Throwing stones Heavy stones and missiles rained from the battlements onto the enemy below.

Loophole Narrow opening through which archers could shoot safely.

Belfry This wheeled tower enabled attackers to reach the top of the wall safely.

Ladder The simplest and quickest way of attacking a castle was to climb the walls using a ladder—the aim was to get a small party inside to open the gates.

Battering ram A large, heavy log, this basic weapon was used to attack walls and gates.

Pavise This wheeled, wooden shield protected attackers from enemy fire.

EXTREME TACTICS

BY CATAPULTING A DISEASE-RIDDEN BODY OVER THE WALLS, ASSAILANTS PUT THE DEFENDERS IN IMMEDIATE PERIL.

DEFENDERS OF A CASTLE COULD SNEAK UP ON THE ENEMY THROUGH A HIDDEN DOORWAY CALLED A SALLY PORT. THE DEFENDING SOLDIERS OF HADLEIGH CASTLE IN ESSEX, U.K., ARE SAID TO HAVE BOMBARDED THEIR ASSAILANTS WITH FRESH FISH THAT THEY HAD SMUGGLED IN.

IN 1306, SCOTLAND'S KILDRUMMY CASTLE FELL TO EDWARD, PRINCE OF WALES, WHEN OSBOURNE, THE TRAITOROUS BLACKSMITH, SET FIRE TO THE CASTLE GRAIN STORE.

IN 1204, FRENCH SOLDIERS TOOK CHÂTEAU GAILLARD FROM ENGLAND'S KING JOHN BY CLIMBING UP THE TOILET CHUTE.

Fame and FORTUNE

Human curiosity is the driving force behind many of history's greatest quests, discoveries, and adventures. People have explored to increase scientific knowledge, spread religious beliefs, gain riches and power, or just out of plain interest. However, many explorers are simply motivated by wealth and fame.

A NEW WORLD

In 1492, **Christopher Columbus** (1451–1506) set sail from Spain in an attempt to find a new route to Asia, to buy spices. When he found land, Columbus thought he'd reached Japan. In fact, he'd found a new continent—the Americas. Upon his return to Spain, the new continent became known as "the New World." In return for his many voyages of discovery, Columbus desired "great rewards" for both himself and his family.

Columbus

HIDDEN HOARD?

Edward Teach (c. 1680–1718), also known as **Blackbeard**, was a ruthless pirate renowned for his deliberately frightening appearance—he even wore slow-burning fuses under his hat. He ambushed and plundered ships in the Caribbean Sea and Atlantic Ocean until he was killed by the Royal Navy. Treasure seekers have since hunted high and low in the hope of finding Teach's legendary buried treasure.

Blackbeard

CUT SHORT

In 1519, Portuguese admiral **Ferdinand Magellan** (1480–1521) set out to travel westward around the world to the Spice Islands, sailing around South America and crossing the Pacific Ocean on the way. The landmark journey made Magellan famous, but he never lived to enjoy it—he was killed by Filipino warriors before his fleet reached its destination.

Magellan

GOLD DIGGER

Most educated Europeans in the 19th century had read Homer's *Iliad* and believed that Troy—one of the cities featured in the poem—was just a legend. From 1871–1873, businessman and amateur archeologist **Heinrich Schliemann** (1822–1890) uncovered the site of Troy at Hissarlik, Turkey. No fewer than nine different cities had been built and destroyed at this spot over the ages. Schliemann also uncovered a hoard of gold jewelry in the process.

EPIC JOURNEY

In *Il Milione*, an autobiographical account about the extraordinary travels of **Marco Polo** (c. 1254–1324), Polo stated that he had not mentioned one half of what he had seen because no one would believe him. In total, he traveled more than 25,000 mi (40,000 km) around the world and discovered many amazing inventions and innovations.

ONE LAST TRY

Howard Carter (1874–1939) was sure that the intact tomb of an ancient pharaoh lay somewhere in Egypt's Valley of the Kings. In 1922, after five years of exploration, Carter's patron, Lord Carnarvon, agreed to fund just one more season of excavation. It was enough —at the end of the year, Carter uncovered the most celebrated archeological find of all time—the tomb of Pharaoh Tutankhamun, untouched since 1327 BC.

PIRATE OR PATRIOT?

Sir Francis Drake (1540–1596) sailed round the world from 1577–1580, attacking Spanish treasure-laden vessels and pillaging their invaluable cargoes. On his return, Drake was hailed a hero and knighted by Queen Elizabeth I for his service to England. In Spain, however, Drake was deemed a murderous pirate.

56 55 54 53 51

43 42 41 36 35 34 33 32

23 24 25 26 27

Schliemann

Carter

Polo

Drake

Wonders
OF THE WORLD

We know about the Seven Wonders of the Ancient World from ancient Greek tourist guides. Historians are in disagreement over which monuments were on the list and even how many actually existed—we may never know for sure because only the Great Pyramid is still standing.

GREAT PYRAMID OF GIZA

WHAT: A giant stone tomb

WHERE: Near Cairo, Egypt

WHEN: Built during the reign of King Khufu (c. 2575-2465 BC)

SIZE: Base 755 sq ft (230 sq m); 480 ft (145 m) high

DESCRIPTION: Orientated on the four points of the compass and containing about 2.3 million limestone blocks, the pyramid was the tomb of King Khufu and his queen. The shape may have been chosen because it points to the sky—the domain of the sun god Ra.

DESCRIPTION: Described as being irrigated by an elaborate system of pumps and channels that brought water from the River Euphrates, the gardens were said to be a leisure feature of the royal palace. One legend says Nebuchadnezzar built them to remind his queen, Amytis, of the green forests of her Persian homeland.

WHAT: Remarkable terraced gardens

WHERE: In Babylon, the capital city of ancient Mesopotamia (now southern Iraq)

WHEN: During the reign of either Queen Sammuramat (810-783 BC) or King Nebuchadnezzar II (c. 605-561 BC)

SIZE: Unknown

HANGING GARDENS OF BABYLON

STATUE OF ZEUS AT OLYMPIA

WHAT: A vast gold and ivory statue

WHERE: Olympia, in the Peloponnese, Greece

WHEN: Constructed by the sculptor Phidias around 430 BC

SIZE: 40 ft (12 m) high

DESCRIPTION: As the Olympic Games had deep religious significance, a temple to the king of the gods adorned the sporting complex. The statue of Zeus was shown seated, giving the impression that if he stood, he would burst through the roof.

TEMPLE OF ARTEMIS AT EPHESUS

DESCRIPTION: Constructed of gleaming white marble, the Temple of Artemis was packed with works of art. Artemis (also known as Diana) was an ancient goddess of the moon. The temple was destroyed in AD 268, rebuilt, and finally razed in AD 401.

WHAT: A gigantic marble-columned temple

WHERE: Ephesus was in modern-day Turkey

WHEN: Built by King Croesus of Lydia c. 550 BC

SIZE: 350 ft (110 m) long, 180 ft (55 m) wide

MAUSOLEUM OF MAUSOLUS AT HALICARNASSUS

DESCRIPTION: The gleaming tomb consisted of a plain rectangular base, topped with a colonnade, a pyramid roof, and a statue of Mausolus and Artemisia in a chariot pulled by four horses. It was built to demonstrate Artemisia's love for her Mausolus, and to glorify them both.

WHAT: A vast tomb shaped like a jewel box

WHERE: Overlooking the ancient city of Halicarnassus (now Bodrum), Turkey

WHEN: Built at the command of Queen Artemisia II of Caria, Mausolus' sister and widow, c. 353–350 BC

SIZE: Square base, with sides about 36 ft (11 m) long; 148 ft (45 m) tall

COLOSSUS OF RHODES

DESCRIPTION: The people of Rhodes erected this mighty bronze and iron statue of the sun god, Helios, to thank the deity for saving their city from enemy attack.

WHAT: A huge statue of a god beside the harbor entrance

WHERE: Mediterranean island of Rhodes, Greece

WHEN: Built 292–280 BC

SIZE: More than 107 ft (30 m) tall

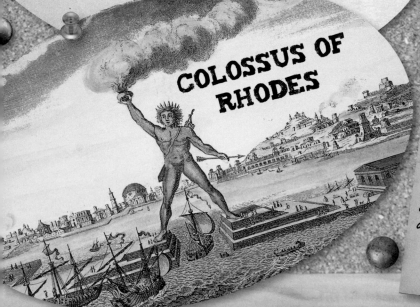

PHAROS OF ALEXANDRIA

DESCRIPTION: The stone building rose in three tapering stages: square, octagonal, and cylindrical. The fire at the top was reflected in mirrors and visible 29 mi (47 km) away—it warned sailors of the treacherous banks around the Nile.

WHAT: The archetypal lighthouse

WHERE: Island of Pharos, Alexandria, Egypt

WHEN: Built 280–247 BC

SIZE: 350 ft (110 m) tall

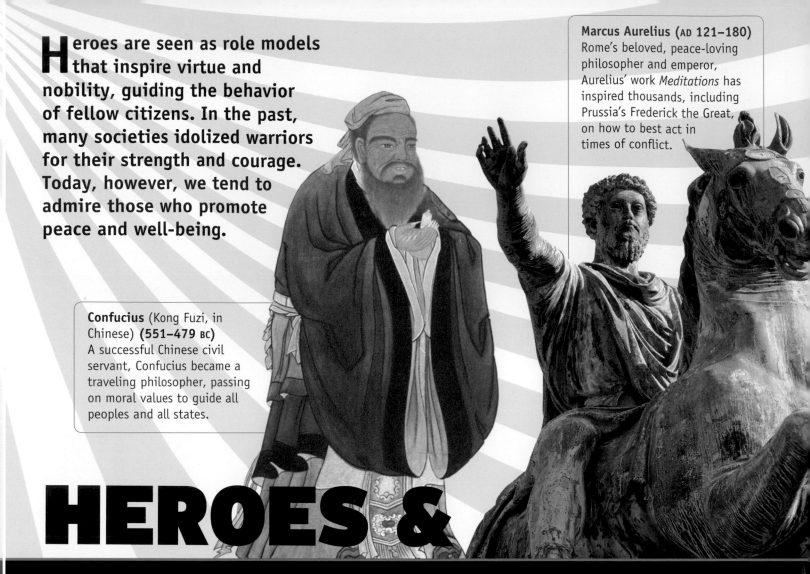

Heroes are seen as role models that inspire virtue and nobility, guiding the behavior of fellow citizens. In the past, many societies idolized warriors for their strength and courage. Today, however, we tend to admire those who promote peace and well-being.

Marcus Aurelius (AD 121–180)
Rome's beloved, peace-loving philosopher and emperor, Aurelius' work *Meditations* has inspired thousands, including Prussia's Frederick the Great, on how to best act in times of conflict.

Confucius (Kong Fuzi, in Chinese) **(551–479 BC)**
A successful Chinese civil servant, Confucius became a traveling philosopher, passing on moral values to guide all peoples and all states.

HEROES &

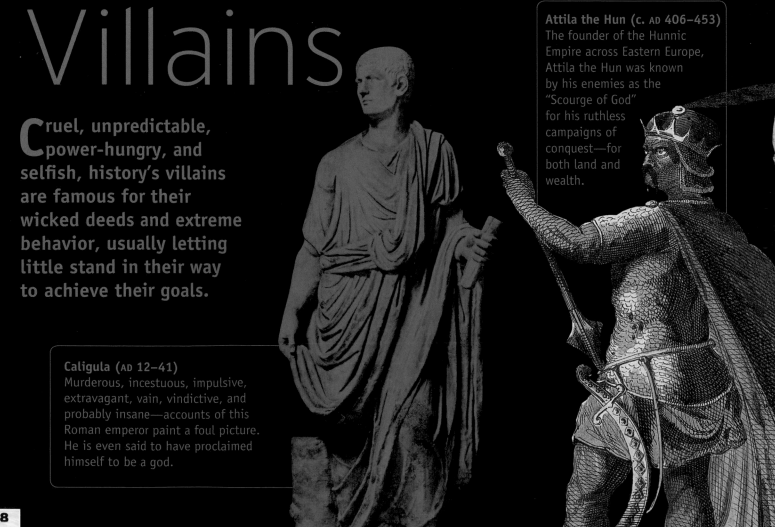

Villains

Cruel, unpredictable, power-hungry, and selfish, history's villains are famous for their wicked deeds and extreme behavior, usually letting little stand in their way to achieve their goals.

Attila the Hun (c. AD 406–453)
The founder of the Hunnic Empire across Eastern Europe, Attila the Hun was known by his enemies as the "Scourge of God" for his ruthless campaigns of conquest—for both land and wealth.

Caligula (AD 12–41)
Murderous, incestuous, impulsive, extravagant, vain, vindictive, and probably insane—accounts of this Roman emperor paint a foul picture. He is even said to have proclaimed himself to be a god.

Abraham Lincoln (1809–1865)
The 16th president of the United States, Lincoln led his nation through the American Civil War (1861–1865) and ended the country's slavery. He was assassinated in 1865 while attending a play with his wife.

Florence Nightingale (1820–1910)
Renowned for her work during the Crimean War (1853–1856), English nurse Nightingale cared for wounded soldiers, known to them as "the lady with the lamp" because she often made her rounds at night. She campaigned for nursing to be accepted as a profession for women.

Nelson Mandela (b. 1918)
In 1948, South Africa implemented a policy of apartheid (forced racial segregation). Mandela was a leader of the resistance movement, and became an international symbol of the fight for tolerance and equality. He was imprisoned for 27 years, and on his release became a respected statesman.

Genghis Khan (c. 1162–1227)
Born a simple tribal leader in northeast Asia, Khan united the nomadic tribes of Mongolia. The self-styled "Universal Ruler" carved out one of the largest empires the world has ever seen—by tireless campaigning and the heartless slaughter of local populations.

Ivan the Terrible (1530–1584)
Russia's first tsar, Ivan IV, became a corrupt and unstable tyrant who massacred thousands and even slew his own son in a fit of rage.

Joseph Stalin (1879–1953)
Born Iosif Dzhugashvili, the leader of the Soviet Union clawed his way to power and then retained the position by means of mass extermination—ordering the death and suffering of millions of people. Stalin is considered to be the force behind the biggest mass murder in history.

Great WARRIORS

Battles were won with the mind as much as muscle. First impressions counted, so warriors who looked intimidating and strong were often victorious. From medieval knights in shining armor to Viking marauders, history's finest fighting men were often extremely successful.

HOPLITE

Category: Citizen infantry
Place of operation: Ancient Greece
Dates: 8th–4th centuries BC
Headgear: Helmet with cheekplates
Body armor: Breastplate and greaves (leg armor), bronze cuirass or linen corselet
Weapons: 8-ft (3-m) spear and short sword
Shield: Round in shape, and made of wood and bronze
Discipline: Good
Notable success: Smashing Persian invasion at Marathon, 490 BC

ROMAN INFANTRY

Category: Professional foot soldier
Place of operation: Europe and the Near East
Dates: 2nd century BC–5th century AD
Headgear: Round, steel helmet with cheekplates
Body armor: Plates over upper body and shoulders
Weapons: 6-ft (2-m) javelin and short sword
Shield: Large, and (after 1st century AD) rectangular and curved. Made of plywood reinforced with bronze or iron
Discipline: Excellent
Notable success: Conquest of Britain, 1st century AD

VIKING

Category: Member of Nordic warrior band. Joined together in later centuries to form large armies
Place of operation: Europe, North Atlantic, and North America
Dates: 8th–11th century
Headgear: Steel helmet (without horns)
Body armor: Leather or chainmail tunic
Weapons: Spear, ax, sword, and dagger
Shield: Small and round. Made of wood or metal
Discipline: Poor
Notable success: Seizing the province of Rouen from the Kingdom of France in AD 911, and renaming it Normandy

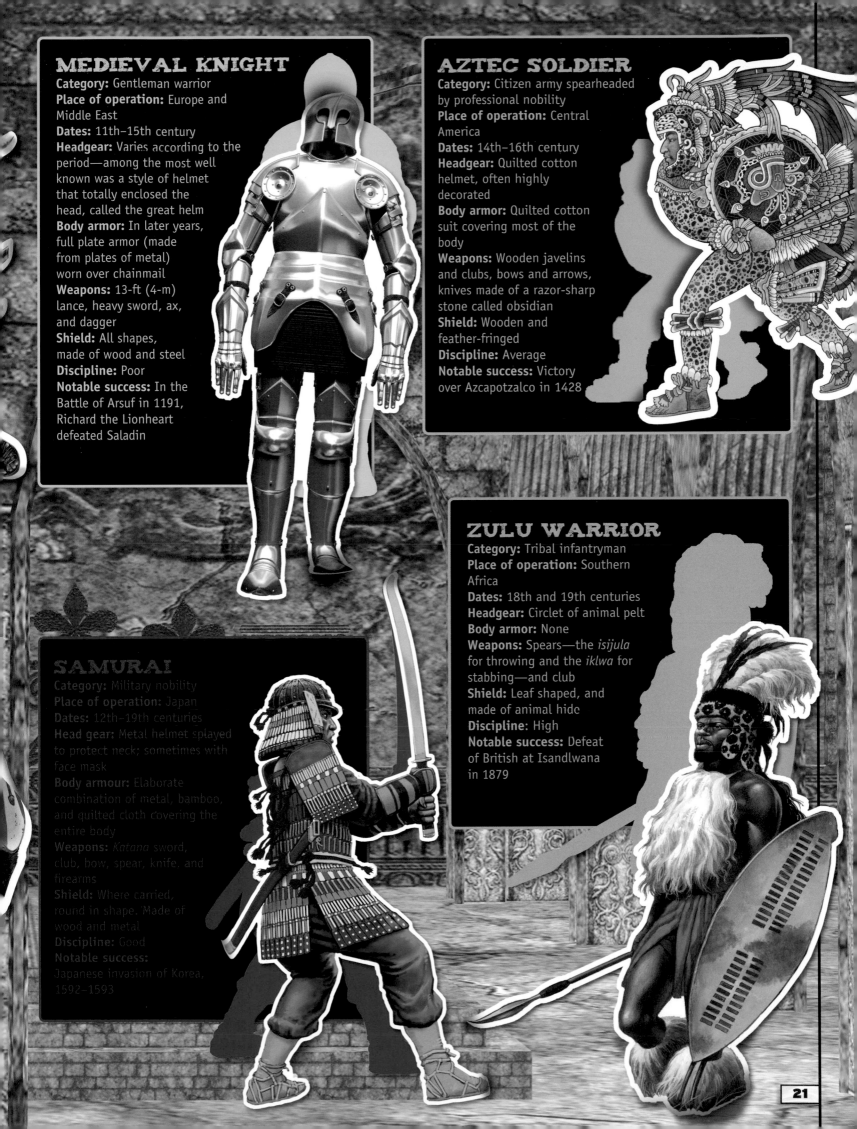

MEDIEVAL KNIGHT

Category: Gentleman warrior
Place of operation: Europe and Middle East
Dates: 11th–15th century
Headgear: Varies according to the period—among the most well known was a style of helmet that totally enclosed the head, called the great helm
Body armor: In later years, full plate armor (made from plates of metal) worn over chainmail
Weapons: 13-ft (4-m) lance, heavy sword, ax, and dagger
Shield: All shapes, made of wood and steel
Discipline: Poor
Notable success: In the Battle of Arsuf in 1191, Richard the Lionheart defeated Saladin

AZTEC SOLDIER

Category: Citizen army spearheaded by professional nobility
Place of operation: Central America
Dates: 14th–16th century
Headgear: Quilted cotton helmet, often highly decorated
Body armor: Quilted cotton suit covering most of the body
Weapons: Wooden javelins and clubs, bows and arrows, knives made of a razor-sharp stone called obsidian
Shield: Wooden and feather-fringed
Discipline: Average
Notable success: Victory over Azcapotzalco in 1428

ZULU WARRIOR

Category: Tribal infantryman
Place of operation: Southern Africa
Dates: 18th and 19th centuries
Headgear: Circlet of animal pelt
Body armor: None
Weapons: Spears—the *isijula* for throwing and the *iklwa* for stabbing—and club
Shield: Leaf shaped, and made of animal hide
Discipline: High
Notable success: Defeat of British at Isandlwana in 1879

SAMURAI

Category: Military nobility
Place of operation: Japan
Dates: 12th–19th centuries
Head gear: Metal helmet splayed to protect neck; sometimes with face mask
Body armour: Elaborate combination of metal, bamboo, and quilted cloth covering the entire body
Weapons: *Katana* sword, club, bow, spear, knife, and firearms
Shield: Where carried, round in shape. Made of wood and metal
Discipline: Good
Notable success: Japanese invasion of Korea, 1592–1593

LOST **LEADERS**

Throughout history, the lives of many key figures—popular and unpopular—have been brought to an untimely close. Assassinations are targeted killings, usually motivated by political differences, but may also be driven by religious beliefs, military opposition, or monetary gain.

French King Henry IV

Fanaticism knows no bounds, as France's popular King Henry IV (1553–1610) discovered in 1610. Born a Protestant, he converted to Catholicism and, to heal his country's religious divisions, granted toleration to those of his former faith. All this was too much for François Ravaillac, who stabbed the king to death when the royal carriage was stopped in busy traffic on the way to the queen's coronation.

Roman general Julius Caesar

The career of one of Rome's greatest generals and reformers, Julius Caesar (100–44 BC), came to an abrupt end on March 15, 44 BC, when he was stabbed to death in the Senate House. The assassins' motive? To save the Roman republic from a would-be king.

ENGLISH KING WILLIAM II

William II (c. 1056–1100) was not one of England's more popular kings. Tongues began to wag, therefore, when he went hunting in the New Forest and did not return. His body, pierced by an arrow, was found the next morning—and his brother Henry immediately seized the throne. Was the king's death an accident, or assassination?

Russian Tsar Alexander II

For all his reforming zeal, notably setting free his country's serfs in 1861, Russian Tsar Alexander II (1818–1881) did not go far enough for the People's Will, an extreme terrorist organization. Whether the people willed it or not, the gang's assassins killed the tsar in a bomb attack as he rode in his carriage through the streets of St. Petersburg.

Austro-Hungarian Archduke Franz Ferdinand

On June 28, 1914, the Serbian nationalist Gavrilo Princip fired two fatal shots in Sarajevo, Bosnia, that started World War I (1914–1918). His victim was the Austro-Hungarian prince, Archduke Franz Ferdinand. Austria soon attacked Serbia. Russia came to the aid of its Serbian ally, and Germany did the same with Austria. France, Russia's ally, was drawn in next... and within weeks a whole continent, then the whole world, was at war.

JFK moments before the shooting took place.

U.S. President John F. Kennedy

As U.S. President John F. Kennedy was driving through Dallas, Texas, U.S., on November 22, 1963, at precisely 12:30 p.m. four shots were fired. The president, hit in the body and head, died shortly afterward. A suspect, Lee Harvey Oswald, was arrested but shot dead before he was brought to trial. So one of modern history's great mysteries began—who killed JFK and why?

Israeli President Yitzhak Rabin

Israel and its Arab neighbors have long been at each other's throats. So when Yitzhak Rabin (1922–1995) signed the Oslo Accords with the Palestinians in 1993, he was awarded the Nobel Prize for Peace. Two years later, he was assassinated by Israeli Yigal Amir who opposed the agreement.

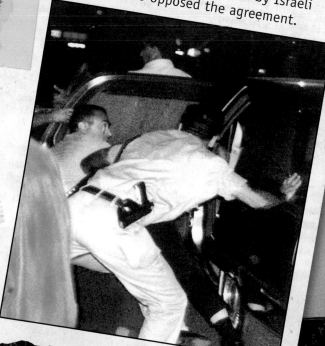

Security agents push Rabin into a car after he was shot in Tel Aviv after addressing a peace rally.

Wipe OUT!

It came from the east, spreading like a wave of death across Europe. In just four years (1347–1351), half of the continent's population was wiped out. Rich and poor, men and women... no one was immune from the bubonic plague, also known as the Great Plague or the "Black Death." Although population levels recovered surprisingly swiftly, the continent would never be the same again.

Spread of death

The Black Death, first brought to Europe by rats aboard vessels sailing from the Eastern Mediterranean, persisted for more than 400 years. Its name came from its most obvious symptoms—pus-oozing, black swellings, called buboes, under the arms, on the neck, and in the groin. Those infected had a one-in-five chance of survival—the majority were dead within a week.

Dirty rats

Most scientists believe the plague was spread by fleas that lived on black rats. In an age when basic hygiene was almost nonexistent, rat fleas flourished in bedding and clothing. It took just one flea bite to infect a person. Modern medics, however, have suggested that the disease was actually caused by a bacterium called *Yersinia pestis*.

This grim depiction shows how people were dying in the street, leaving piles of diseased bodies.

Doctor, doctor

At a time when some doctors believed the plague could be spread by just looking at someone, so-called "cures" were bizarre. They included swallowing emeralds, pearls, or gold, placing dried human excrement on the buboes, and drinking a mixture of apple syrup, lemon, rose water, and peppermint.

▶ Doctors wore "plague-proof clothing." The "beak" acted like a gas mask, stopping them from inhaling air that may carry the plague when treating victims.

ONE MEDIEVAL REMEDY FOR THE PLAGUE WAS TO DRINK A GLASS OF YOUR OWN URINE TWICE A DAY.

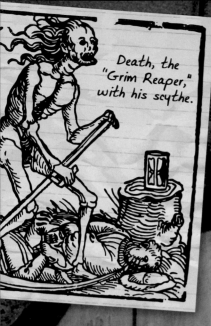
Death, the "Grim Reaper," with his scythe.

Mass graves

The bodies of plague victims had to be disposed of as quickly as possible, otherwise the bodies would rot and spread further disease. With so many deaths, individual funerals were impossible. Corpses were simply collected in carts and dumped in mass graves.

► Hundreds of dead bodies were buried in pits.

Heaven's judgment

In a fiercely religious age, the plague was seen as God's judgment on a wicked world. Prevention and cure came not from science, but from prayer, confession, and penance.

▼ More than 1,000 bodies were discovered in Black Death graves near the Tower of London, England, in 1987.

Flagellation (beating or whipping the body) was believed to atone for the sins that had brought the plague.

On and on...

Evidence of the dreadful Black Death has come from the excavation of mass graves. Outbreaks of this terrifying epidemic have also occured in modern times—as recently as 1994 there was an outbreak in Seurat, India.

Supreme
SACRIFICE

The early gods were a grim bunch. Erratic and demanding, a number of them could be appeased only with the ultimate sacrifice—human life. No one did this in a more spectacularly gory fashion than the Aztec people of what is now southern Mexico.

▲ An Aztec priest cuts out the beating heart of a prisoner of war and holds it up to the sun god.

Burning basket

When campaigning in Northern Europe, Julius Caesar described how Celtic druids pleased their gods with human sacrifice. He reported that they had built a huge, wickerwork statue, imprisoned people within it, and then set fire to the structure.

▶ According to Caesar, the criminal and innocent alike were sacrificed within the large, wicker statue.

Heart of the matter

The Aztecs believed that Huitzilopochtli, the god of war and sun, needed a regular supply of blood to sustain him in his battle with darkness. Therefore, on festive days, prisoners of war were taken to the sacrificial altar atop the pyramid temple in Tenochtitlan, the capital of the Aztec Empire. Here, the hearts of victims were cut out in a bloody ritual.

Sati is the ancient Hindu custom of burning a bereaved wife on the funeral pyre of her dead husband.

Pyre power

The Hindu ritual, Sati, demanded that a wife be burned to death, voluntarily or otherwise, on the funeral pyre of her dead husband. It was believed that the custom arose to stop young wives poisoning elderly and unwanted husbands.

GREEK MYTHS TELL HOW EVERY SEVEN YEARS THE ATHENIANS SENT 14 CHILDREN TO BE EATEN BY THE MINOTAUR, A TERRIFYING MONSTER.

Pleasing Thor

According to the medieval German chronicler Adam of Bremen, the ancient temple at Uppsala, Sweden, witnessed some pretty grim events. The worship of Thor and other Norse gods and goddesses involved ritual human sacrifice.

The Nordic King Domalde prepares to sacrifice himself for the good of his people.

A Japanese kamikaze plane attempts to smash into a U.S. warship.

Divine wind

The term "kamikaze," meaning "divine wind," was originally used to describe the tropical typhoons that broke up Chinese invasion fleets heading for Japan in the late 13th century. In World War II, the term was adopted by Japanese suicide pilots who deliberately smashed their planes into U.S. warships—about 2,800 kamikaze attacks sank or crippled hundreds of ships.

FANCY DRESS

As soon as our ancestors started wearing clothing more than 100,000 years ago, they wanted to look good. Most garments were attractive and designed to accentuate the wearer's best features. But at the extremes, people's fashion obsessions became peculiar—for example, women piling their hair 12 in (30 cm) high. Some fashion trends were even cruel, such as the Chinese practice of binding girls' feet so they could fit into shoes many sizes too small for them.

◄▼ The toga was both a garment and a badge of citizenship.

Roman robe

The toga of ancient Rome was much more than a simple 20-ft- (6-m-) long robe of fine wool, draped around the body and slung over the shoulder. It also showed the wearer's place in society—by law, the garment could be worn only by male citizens of Rome.

◄ Proud of a shapely leg, 16th-century men wore tights to show theirs off.

Elizabethan costume

Shakespeare's theater company's most valuable possession was its wardrobe of costumes. Not surprisingly, it cost more than most Elizabethans earned in a year to dress a gentleman in a lined, embroidered doublet (jacket) with detachable sleeves, neck ruff, padded tights over the upper thigh and silk stockings below, and elegant shoes.

Geisha girls

Since the 18th century, highly trained Japanese Geisha have been used for entertainment. With a chalk-white face, scarlet lips, hair decorated with flowers, an elegant kimono, a brilliant obi (sash), and platform shoes, a Geisha captivated her guests with elaborate dance and music.

◄ Geishas still work today, attending parties and gatherings.

Aristocratic excess

▶ Costumes in the 18th century were low at the front and high on the head.

Late 18th-century European dress is a fabulous example of fashion at its most extreme. A lady's gown ballooned like a bell from her tiny waist, and the puffed sleeves were trimmed with ruffles. The hairdo, many times the size of the wearer's head, looked like a bird had made its nest atop the entire extraordinary collection.

▼ The marked faces of New Zealand's Maori warriors made them look ferocious.

Bone-cut beauty

The Maori people of New Zealand boasted a long tradition of Tā moko, marking the body permanently with incisions and natural dyes. Carved with bone chisels, the markings were used to indicate power and authority. They appeared most commonly on the face, thighs, and buttocks.

Remarkable rears

Late 19th-century fashion designers created bustle dresses that expanded so much at the rear, they had to be supported by steel cages.

◀ The bustle dress exaggerated a woman's rear to make her appear more attractive.

Eagle signals

When in battle, an opponent knew immediately whether to fight or flee from a Native American Sioux, Crow, Blackfeet, Cheyenne, or Plains Cree warrior. Each eagle feather in the striking warbonnet of a warrior represented an act of outstanding bravery. Lots of feathers? Get out of the way—fast!

◀ The feathers in the warbonnet of Sitting Bull, the war chief of the Sioux, continued down his back.

RAT-atouille

H umans are omnivorous—we eat both plants and meat. During the reign of England's James I (1603–1625), starving soldiers resorted to sharing the diet of their cows—grass. At the other extreme, Henry VIII (1491–1547) sat down to vast feasts of hare, venison, veal, chicken, plums, and pomegranate seeds... and that was just the first course!

DURING THE CIVIL WAR THAT FOLLOWED THE RUSSIAN REVOLUTION OF 1917, STARVING PEASANTS WERE PHOTOGRAPHED SELLING HUMAN FLESH FOR PEOPLE TO EAT.

GREEDY ROMANS SOMETIMES MADE THEMSELVES SICK IN ORDER TO BE ABLE TO EAT MORE.

Hand to mouth
For most of history, people used knives to cut meat and spoons to scoop up liquid, but they generally used their fingers to transfer food to their mouths. Fine if your hands are clean...

Extreme generosity
In 1900, the French government employed 3,600 cooks and waiters to prepare a feast for the country's mayors that featured, among other things, more than 2 tons of pheasant and 50,000 bottles of wine. Bon appétit!

LITTLE LUXURY

Ancient Romans were partial to a mid-morning snack, and one of their favorite nibbles was a crunchy edible dormouse.

A feast of beasts

Chronicles say that around 484 BC, King Darius of Persia had 1,000 animals slaughtered for a special feast. The menu was said to have included smoked camel, ox, zebra, and ostrich.

Big bird

Until the 17th century, swan was a popular dish among the wealthiest in society. The bird was roasted for a long time and served "like beef."

Raise a glass?

Before the late 16th century, most Europeans drank their tipple from pewter, pottery, or leather. Drinking vessels made from leather were lined with resin to make them watertight.

Boozy breakfast

In medieval times, water and milk frequently carried diseases. To avoid illness, those who could afford to drank beer and wine at all times of the day and night.

Fitting the CRIME

Legal systems claim that a person's punishment should fit their crime. Yet from hanging for stealing a sheep to crushing bones for lifting a loaf, the past is littered with examples of extreme punishments given out for apparently trivial crimes.

Off with his head

One of the most shocking punishments took place during the French Revolution's Reign of Terror (1793–1794). Once the revolutionary leader Maximilien Robespierre had defined the crime—being an enemy of the people, and the punishment—death, thousands of men and women were guillotined for the crime of simply being who they were. An aristocrat, for instance, was by definition an enemy of the people.

GET OUT!

The ancient Athenians devised a fail-safe way of dealing with those who were regarded as a political nuisance. A meeting of citizens was called, at which all present wrote on a potsherd (a fragment of pottery, called an *ostrakon*) the name of anyone they wished to remove. Anyone receiving a large number of votes was ostracized—banished from the state for ten years.

▼ The name of an unpopular Athenian citizen is scratched onto a piece of pottery.

► In the late 18th century, the iron maiden was used as a form of torture. The victim was shut inside the cabinet and pierced with sharp objects.

In 1793, Marie Antoinette was executed by guillotine for treason.

TOOLS OF TORTURE

Torture has long been a means of extracting information from a person—usually using brutal methods. There was no question of punishments fitting the crime for slaves in ancient Rome. In the pre-Christian era, slaves accused of a crime, even a minor one, were automatically tortured—it was seen as the only way of getting the truth out of them. Harsher still, in imperial times, when a slave was found guilty of murder, it was quite common for all other slaves belonging to the same master to be crucified.

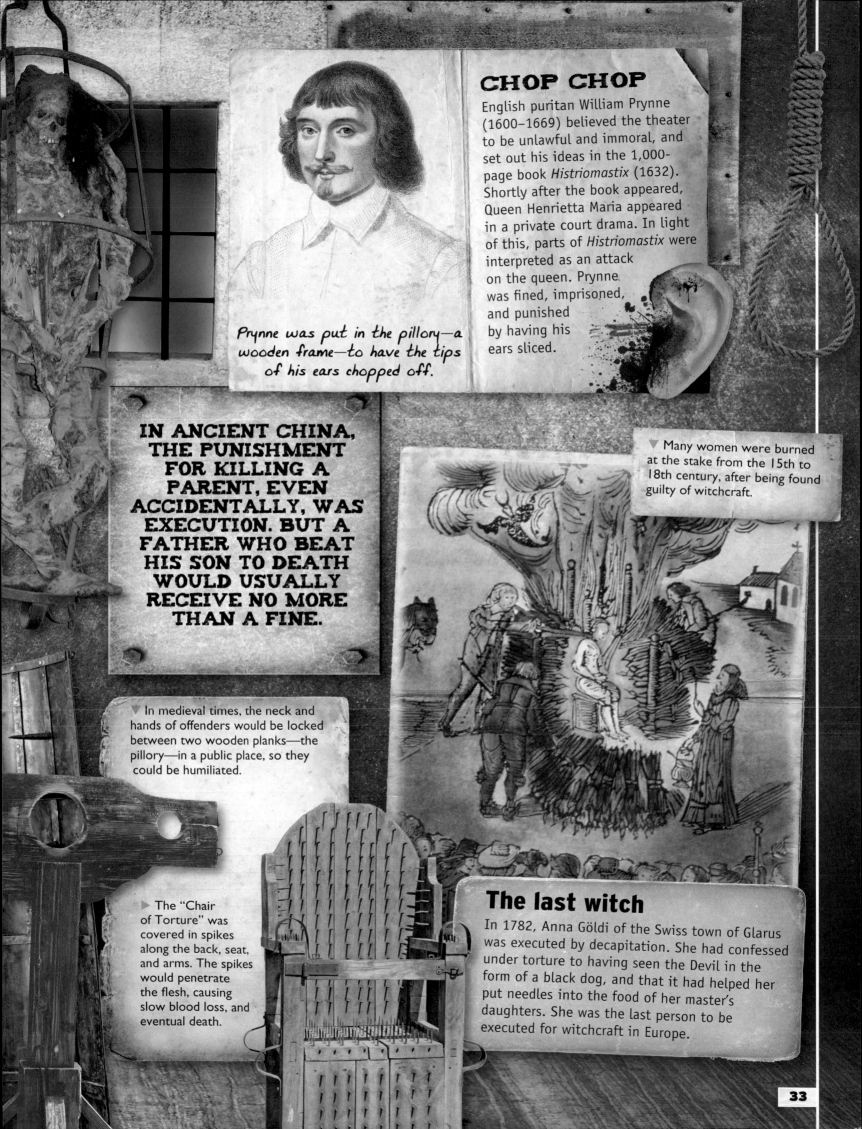

CHOP CHOP

English puritan William Prynne (1600–1669) believed the theater to be unlawful and immoral, and set out his ideas in the 1,000-page book *Histriomastix* (1632). Shortly after the book appeared, Queen Henrietta Maria appeared in a private court drama. In light of this, parts of *Histriomastix* were interpreted as an attack on the queen. Prynne was fined, imprisoned, and punished by having his ears sliced.

Prynne was put in the pillory—a wooden frame—to have the tips of his ears chopped off.

IN ANCIENT CHINA, THE PUNISHMENT FOR KILLING A PARENT, EVEN ACCIDENTALLY, WAS EXECUTION. BUT A FATHER WHO BEAT HIS SON TO DEATH WOULD USUALLY RECEIVE NO MORE THAN A FINE.

▼ Many women were burned at the stake from the 15th to 18th century, after being found guilty of witchcraft.

▼ In medieval times, the neck and hands of offenders would be locked between two wooden planks—the pillory—in a public place, so they could be humiliated.

▶ The "Chair of Torture" was covered in spikes along the back, seat, and arms. The spikes would penetrate the flesh, causing slow blood loss, and eventual death.

The last witch

In 1782, Anna Göldi of the Swiss town of Glarus was executed by decapitation. She had confessed under torture to having seen the Devil in the form of a black dog, and that it had helped her put needles into the food of her master's daughters. She was the last person to be executed for witchcraft in Europe.

Cure
OR KILL

Until the scientific revolution of the late 17th century, most medicine was a mix of superstition, religion, folklore, myth, trickery, and guesswork. "Cures" included rubbing the affected part of the body with a live toad (a treatment for the plague), drinking a cup of tea made from ground-up insects (antirabies medicine), and dressing a wound with a scribe's excrement and milk. Many so-called treatments did more harm than good, and those who stayed out of the hands of doctors often had the best chance of survival!

MEDIEVAL MEDICINE WAS BASED ON THE IDEA THAT THE BODY CONTAINED FOUR "HUMORS"—BLACK BILE, YELLOW BILE, PHLEGM, AND BLOOD. AN EXCESS OF BLACK BILE, FOR EXAMPLE, WAS THOUGHT TO PRODUCE MELANCHOLY.

FEELING THE HEAT

A person suffering from toothache in medieval Europe may be instructed to hold a lit candle close to the affected area. Apparently this would cause the worms that were eating away the inside of the tooth to drop out into a waiting cup.

Burning away the badness: curing toothache with a lit candle.

Cure by hot cups in a German bathhouse.

TOXIN TREATMENT

The traditional treatment of placing hot cups on the skin has been used since the time of the ancient Egyptians. This "cure" is intended to draw unwanted fluids from the body as the air inside the cups cools and contracts. The procedure creates circular marks on the skin and has no proven benefits.

Cups are still used today in alternative medicine.

PENNY DREADFUL

Not until modern times was mental illness properly recognized or treated. Until the 19th century, London's Bethlem Royal Hospital (once known as Bedlam) was a kind of freak show where visitors paid a penny to gawp at unfortunate "mad" inmates held in chains.

◀ The well-dressed women in this scene from *A Rake's Progress* by 18th-century English artist William Hogarth are visiting Bedlam (London's hospital for the mentally ill) as entertainment.

Self-medication with the help of bloodsucking leeches.

LOSING A LIMB

A mangled or seriously septic limb is better off than on. But before the invention of anesthetic, such operations (usually performed with dirty knives or saws) often led to the conscious patient's immediate death—from shock.

This may hurt a bit... amputation, 17th-century style.

BLOODSUCKERS

Many prescientific societies believed that removing blood from the body, either via an incision into a vein or by drawing it out using leeches, helped to cure illness. In fact, apart from temporarily relieving high blood pressure, this treatment made the patient worse.

DOCTOR TOAD

In medieval times people wore small bags around their necks. Inside would be a dustlike substance, which was believed to ward off all kinds of illnesses, even cancer. The "miracle" cure? Dried and powdered toad.

Get ready to grind: powdered toad acts as a "miracle" cure.

Hole in the head

All over the world, from prehistoric times onward, head injuries, migraines, and even depression were treated by "trepanning"—an operation in which a hole up to 2 in (5 cm) across was drilled in the skull to relieve pressure or let out excess fluid. The procedure did save some lives, but the risk of death by fatal infection or surgeon's error was high.

◄ Trepanning caused as many headaches as it cured.

An unlucky patient with a holey head.

There have always been rich and poor people, but when the Industrial Revolution began in the mid-18th century—first in Britain, then spreading to Europe, North America, and eventually the rest of the world—this gulf became more obvious. Workers who swarmed into cities lived in makeshift, squalid housing, while across the ocean, transported Africans endured even worse conditions as unpaid slaves. All the while, thousands of mill and mine owners, bankers, shippers, and builders were growing rich beyond their wildest dreams.

All in one room

Until the 20th century, it was quite common for European working-class families to have no more than a single room to live in. The situation was especially bad in the rapidly expanding industrial cities.

▲ It was common for large families to live, sleep, and eat in just one room.

SLUMDOGS and

MILLIONAIRES

Royal riches

Queen Victoria received £385,000 a year from the British government just for being queen. That's equivalent to £21 million, or $34 million in today's money. When she died in 1901, she left a fortune of over £2 million (about £24 million, or $50 million today).

THE DUKE OF PORTLAND HAD A 1.5-MI (2.4-KM) UNDERGROUND TUNNEL BUILT SO HE COULD TRAVEL FROM HIS HOME (WELBECK ABBEY, U.K.) TO THE RAILWAY STATION AT WORKSOP WITHOUT BEING SEEN.

NO EXPENSE SPARED—
THE CORONATION OF QUEEN
VICTORIA (1838) COST £70,000.

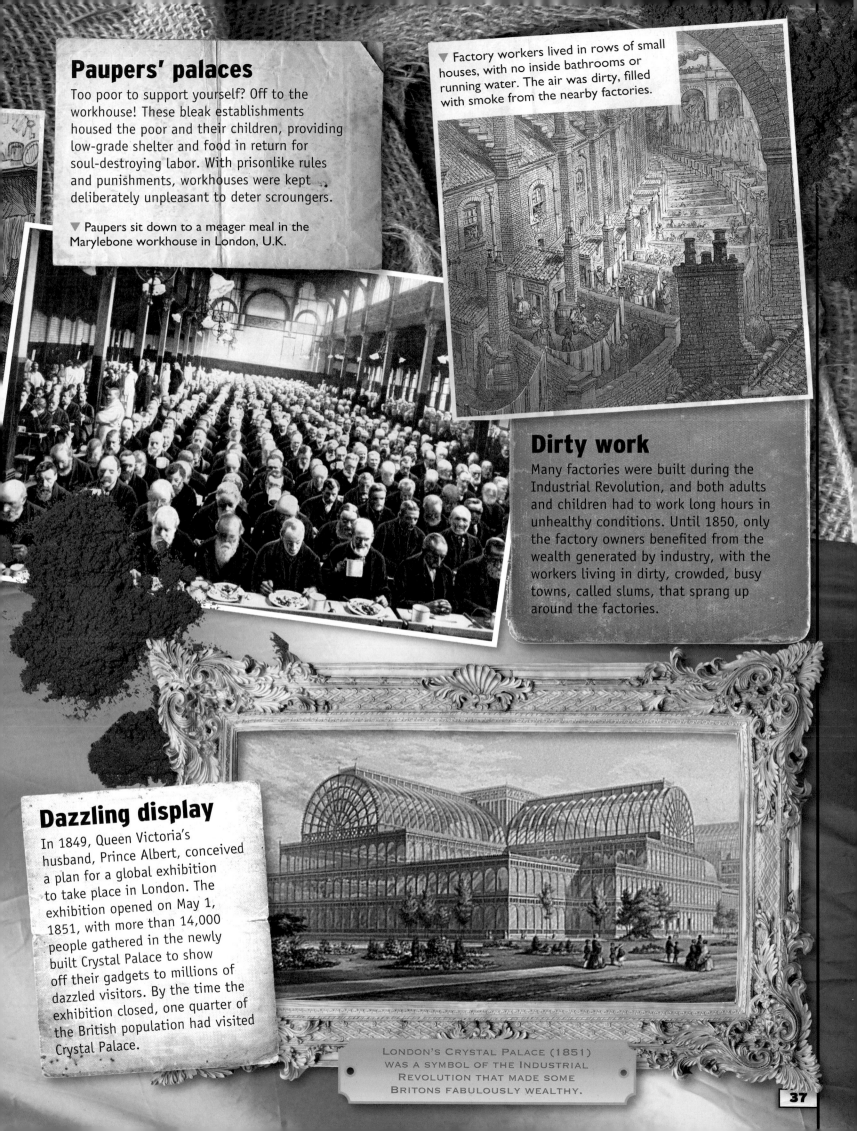

Paupers' palaces

Too poor to support yourself? Off to the workhouse! These bleak establishments housed the poor and their children, providing low-grade shelter and food in return for soul-destroying labor. With prisonlike rules and punishments, workhouses were kept deliberately unpleasant to deter scroungers.

▼ Paupers sit down to a meager meal in the Marylebone workhouse in London, U.K.

▼ Factory workers lived in rows of small houses, with no inside bathrooms or running water. The air was dirty, filled with smoke from the nearby factories.

Dirty work

Many factories were built during the Industrial Revolution, and both adults and children had to work long hours in unhealthy conditions. Until 1850, only the factory owners benefited from the wealth generated by industry, with the workers living in dirty, crowded, busy towns, called slums, that sprang up around the factories.

Dazzling display

In 1849, Queen Victoria's husband, Prince Albert, conceived a plan for a global exhibition to take place in London. The exhibition opened on May 1, 1851, with more than 14,000 people gathered in the newly built Crystal Palace to show off their gadgets to millions of dazzled visitors. By the time the exhibition closed, one quarter of the British population had visited Crystal Palace.

LONDON'S CRYSTAL PALACE (1851) WAS A SYMBOL OF THE INDUSTRIAL REVOLUTION THAT MADE SOME BRITONS FABULOUSLY WEALTHY.

WAR AND PEACE

Prince of peace

Horrified by the 100,000 casualties resulting from the Kalinga War (c. 265 BC), the great Indian emperor Ashoka (304–232 BC) converted to Buddhism and inaugurated one of the most peaceful, fair, and tolerant reigns history has ever witnessed. Education, health, justice, welfare—every branch of government felt the touch of his nonviolent outlook. After Ashoka's death, he was remembered as Samraat Chakravartin—the Emperor of Emperors.

Humans, said the poet Alexander Pope, are "The glory, jest, and riddle of the world"—and never more so than in matters of war and peace. After the horrors of World War I (1914–1918), monuments to peace went up all over Europe; yet barely 20 years later the continent was tearing itself apart once again. Although many of history's most celebrated figures were promoters of peace, we also have a fascination with the heroic (and sometimes barbaric) deeds of warriors and military leaders.

A reputation for destruction

Hollywood has made a pretty good job of portraying the Roman Empire as a place of war and gratuitous violence, but this picture is unfair. For over 200 years (AD 27–180) the empire fought few major wars and spread a relatively civilized blanket of law and order across the Mediterranean world, over which it held sway.

Many people's views of the Roman Empire are informed by movies such as *Gladiator* (2000), which emphasize its violence rather than its imposition of law and order.

Land grab

In 1066, William of Normandy seized the English crown and so began a conflict that finally ended in 1558, when Calais, England's last continental possession, fell to the French. Essentially, the struggle was dynastic—fueled by kings trying to expand their territories by force rather than ethical issues. This unworthy conflict reached its climax in the Hundred Years' War (which actually lasted for 116 years, 1337–1453).

◀ French, Spanish, and English forces battle for power at Nájera, in 1367.

Stacks of skulls

The central Asian conqueror Tamerlane (1336–1405) specialized in acts of extreme barbarity. While carving out an empire around Persia and the Caspian Sea, his forces may have killed 100,000 innocent citizens in a single day. On a more personal note, he took pleasure in firing human heads from cannon, and built huge pyramids from the skulls of his victims.

▶ Ruthless conqueror Tamerlane was also known as "Amir Timur" or (inaccurately) "Timur the Great."

Ultimate weapon

On August 6, 1945, the atom bomb nicknamed "Little Boy" obliterated the Japanese city of Hiroshima, and humankind saw that it now had the power to destroy itself and the planet on which it lived. U.S. President Harry S. Truman had thought long and hard about using the bomb, eventually deciding that dropping it would, in the long run, save lives. We all live with the consequences of that decision.

▲ Hiroshima, 1945: the utter devastation provides a stark warning to humanity.

Crazy ACTS

When Mr. Bumble declared in Charles Dickens' *Oliver Twist*, "The law is an ass!" he was not so far off the mark. History is littered with ill-considered laws, and while some were merely foolish, others were downright nasty. An English law banning entry into Parliament in full armor might have made sense in 1313, but was still on the statute book in 2011. A law passed in 1908 in the U.S. state of Oklahoma banned marriage between a "person of African descent" and "any person not of African descent."

Lean and mean

Debates about obesity often present it as a modern issue. However, an English law of 1336, designed to prevent the population from becoming fat and unfit, made it illegal to eat more than two courses at a single meal.

The "Rich Kitchen" by Jan van der Heyden, 1563.

Crazy cabs

The rules and regulations for taxicabs are very specific. In London, U.K., it is illegal to hail a taxicab if you are suffering from the plague. Furthermore, it is forbidden for a taxicab to carry corpses or rabid dogs.

Single or married?

In Florida, U.S., an unmarried woman may face jail if she parachutes on a Sunday. In Vermont, U.S., a husband must give written permission for his wife to be allowed to wear false teeth.

Dressing up

Lawmakers love to interfere in daily life, especially when it comes to dress. The Italian capital Rome banned low-cut dresses during the 16th century, and in Massachusetts, U.S., a law of 1651 outlawed the wearing of gold or silver buttons, lace, and other finery by anyone not worth at least £200.

Mulberry madness

China ferociously guarded its hold over the immensely profitable silk industry, and punished anyone who let slip the top-secret processes involved. One law stated that any person who revealed how the cocoons of the larvae of the mulberry silkworm were harvested and turned into thread would be put to death by torture.

The power of names

Although he was an undemocratic dictator, the people of France had huge admiration for Emperor Napoleon I (1769–1821)—so much so that they made it illegal to name a pig after him. The move inspired English writer George Orwell to use the name for the tyrannous pig in his book *Animal Farm* (1945).

Loony law

A law allegedly passed by an absentminded U.S. state of Florida legislature in the 1960s made it illegal to carry firearms "except for the purpose of shooting vermin or policemen in the course of their duty." The wording was amended before a law officer was harmed.

▼ Black passengers on a South African train give the thumbs up from a carriage that was previously reserved for white people only.

SLEGS BLANKES
EUROPEANS ONLY

Racist rot

Having legislated to define everyone by their race, in 1950 the South African government passed a law (the Group Areas Act) stipulating where members of each racial group were allowed to live. Needless to say, the white sections of society, who had made the law, were allocated the best areas.

Unearth HISTORY

Dig deeper into the mysteries of the past. From ancient artifacts to lost cities, uncover a forgotten world.

◄ Hundreds of terra-cotta soldiers, horses, and chariots were discovered in Shandong, China, in 2002. The soldiers were once painted in bright colors.

ACCIDENTAL Finds

The discovery of an ancient site helps archeologists to uncover the past. Sometimes ordinary people come face to face with history unexpectedly. A farmer may uncover Egyptian pottery, a caver may stumble across Native American arrowheads, or a metal detector may find a hoard of Roman silver. Each piece gives an insight into the history of human life.

THE FACE OF POWER

The Crosby Garrett helmet was found in 2010 in Cumbria, England, using a metal detector. It dates back to between the 1st and 3rd centuries AD. This brass cavalry helmet would never have been practical for the battlefield. It was probably made for the parade ground, or for public ceremonies. The face acted as a visor and the wearer would have struck awe into all who saw him, his face shining like a god.

A SHIP IN MANHATTAN

In 2010, workers building the new World Trade Center in New York City, U.S., uncovered the remains of a wooden ship, with a hull that was 32.2 ft (9.8 m) long. Tests on the wood showed that it dates back to the 1770s, the time of the American Revolution. The sailing ship was a locally built sloop. It had probably traded up and down the Hudson River or along the coast.

SAXON GOLD

In 2009, a metal detector made an incredible discovery—the Staffordshire Hoard. It included more than 3,500 items of gold, silver, and garnets. The artifacts date back to the 7th or 8th century—the time of the kingdom of Mercia. This hoard is the largest collection of Anglo-Saxon gold and silver ever found.

Sacred scrolls

From 1946 to 1947, two shepherds living near the shores of the Dead Sea, Palestine, discovered precious scrolls in some ancient caves. By 1956, 972 separate texts had been identified. They were written between 150 BC and AD 70 and include parts of the Hebrew Bible and other writings about religious sects.

A Roman piggy bank

In 2010, a pottery jar was uncovered by metal detecting in Frome, England. It contained 52,503 Roman coins, dating from AD 253–305. Many of the coins were from the time of Carausius, an army commander who proclaimed himself of Celtic origin breakaway Roman emperor in AD 286.

PLANNING A DIG

Archeological digs are carried out by museums, universities, and historical societies. Digs can often last for months. Archeologists and volunteers use special tools so as not to damage any of the finds during excavation.

LEGENDARY Prizes

Schliemann found this stunning gold mask at Mycenae in Greece.

The greatest archeological finds can change the way we think about the past. Some explorers have devoted many years of their lives to searching for the ultimate sites. Significant discoveries may be in challenging locations, massive in size, incredibly ancient, or even solve a historical puzzle.

Monster move

The big dig—this is the site of Kalhu or Nimrud, in modern Iraq. Here stood the splendid palace of King Ashurnasirpal II, who ruled the Assyrian Empire from 883 to 859 BC. Inside were giant statues of lions and winged bulls with human heads, to guard the king against evil. In 1847 archeologist Austen Henry Layard (1817–1894) decided to move two of these to the British Museum in London, U.K.

Each giant statue weighed about 10 tons. It took 300 men to haul them to the bank of the River Tigris—an epic task!

ALONG WITH THE TERRA-COTTA ARMY, 11 TERRA-COTTA ACROBATS AND STRONGMEN WERE UNCOVERED.

▲ A bearded human head, wearing a sacred headdress, tops the 13-ft- (4-m-) high winged bull statue.

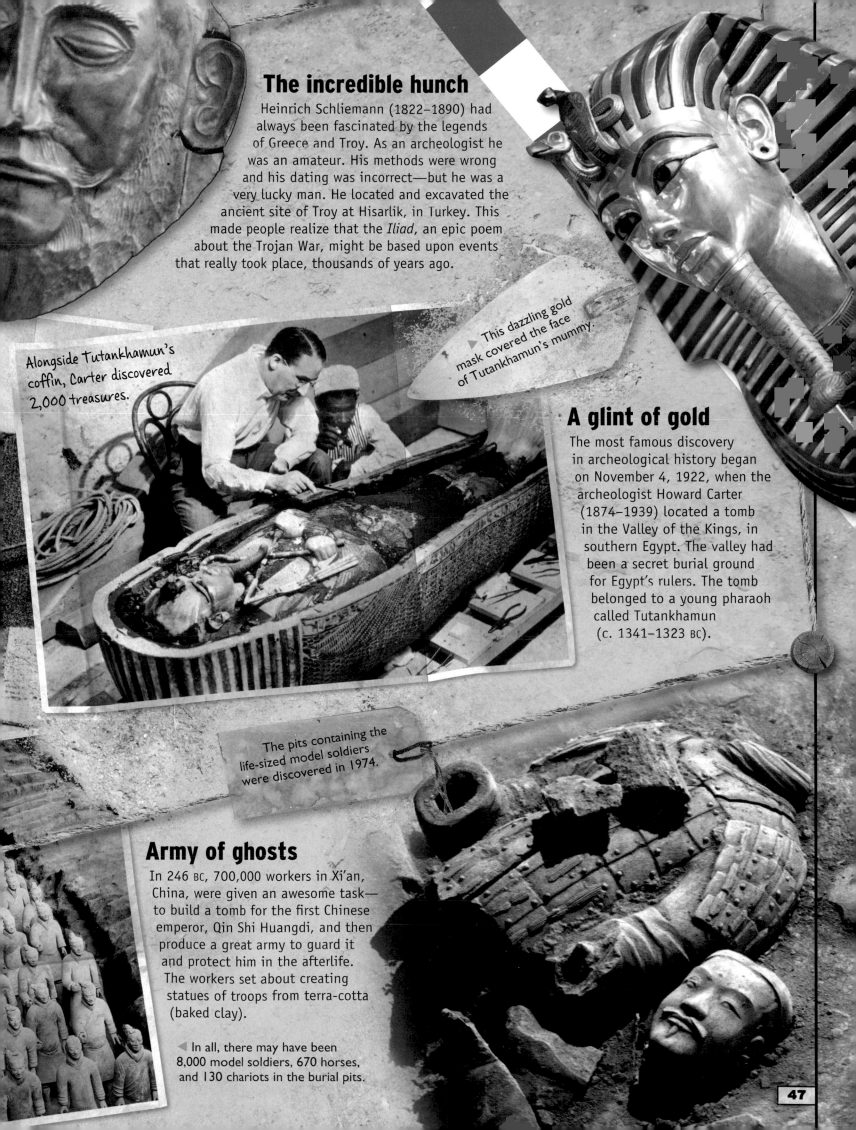

The incredible hunch

Heinrich Schliemann (1822–1890) had always been fascinated by the legends of Greece and Troy. As an archeologist he was an amateur. His methods were wrong and his dating was incorrect—but he was a very lucky man. He located and excavated the ancient site of Troy at Hisarlik, in Turkey. This made people realize that the *Iliad*, an epic poem about the Trojan War, might be based upon events that really took place, thousands of years ago.

Alongside Tutankhamun's coffin, Carter discovered 2,000 treasures.

▶ This dazzling gold mask covered the face of Tutankhamun's mummy.

A glint of gold

The most famous discovery in archeological history began on November 4, 1922, when the archeologist Howard Carter (1874–1939) located a tomb in the Valley of the Kings, in southern Egypt. The valley had been a secret burial ground for Egypt's rulers. The tomb belonged to a young pharaoh called Tutankhamun (c. 1341–1323 BC).

The pits containing the life-sized model soldiers were discovered in 1974.

Army of ghosts

In 246 BC, 700,000 workers in Xi'an, China, were given an awesome task— to build a tomb for the first Chinese emperor, Qin Shi Huangdi, and then produce a great army to guard it and protect him in the afterlife. The workers set about creating statues of troops from terra-cotta (baked clay).

◀ In all, there may have been 8,000 model soldiers, 670 horses, and 130 chariots in the burial pits.

MIGHTY Monuments

Throughout history, people have raised massive buildings, monuments, and statues. The builder's aim has been to create a sense of respect, terror, wonder, or delight. For archeologists, they help to show how past societies lived.

TEMPLE OF THE SERPENT

Chichén Itzá in Mexico was a great city of the Maya and Toltec peoples, occupied between the 8th and 13th centuries AD. In its later years, a great stepped pyramid was built there as a temple to the Feathered Serpent god. A snake, carved in stone, adorns the stairways, and twice each year the Sun casts strange snakelike shadows on the northern steps. The monument later became known in Spanish as *el Castillo*, meaning "the Castle."

Chartres Cathedral

The glorious Rose Window at Chartres Cathedral in France was built around 1215.

Chichén Itzá

The pyramid and its platform have one step for each day of the year.

ISLAND GUARDIANS

The first European seafarers to reach the coasts of the remote Pacific island of Rapa Nui ("Easter Island") were mystified by huge stone statues, called Moai. They were carved by the Polynesians who lived there between 1200 and 1680. The tallest statue is 33 ft (10 m) high and the heaviest weighs 86 tons.

EASTER ISLAND MOAI

887 Moai have survived on Easter Island. They represent ancestors who became gods.

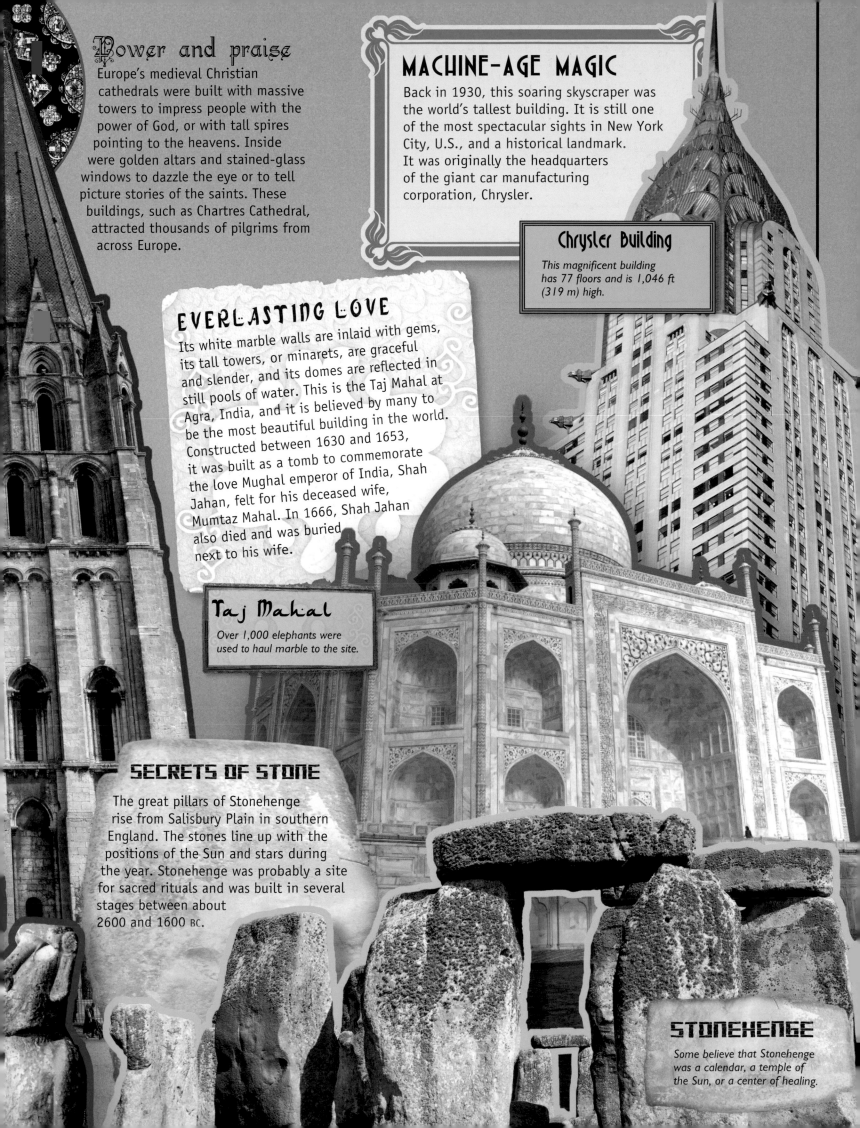

Power and praise

Europe's medieval Christian cathedrals were built with massive towers to impress people with the power of God, or with tall spires pointing to the heavens. Inside were golden altars and stained-glass windows to dazzle the eye or to tell picture stories of the saints. These buildings, such as Chartres Cathedral, attracted thousands of pilgrims from across Europe.

MACHINE-AGE MAGIC

Back in 1930, this soaring skyscraper was the world's tallest building. It is still one of the most spectacular sights in New York City, U.S., and a historical landmark. It was originally the headquarters of the giant car manufacturing corporation, Chrysler.

Chrysler Building

This magnificent building has 77 floors and is 1,046 ft (319 m) high.

EVERLASTING LOVE

Its white marble walls are inlaid with gems, its tall towers, or minarets, are graceful and slender, and its domes are reflected in still pools of water. This is the Taj Mahal at Agra, India, and it is believed by many to be the most beautiful building in the world. Constructed between 1630 and 1653, it was built as a tomb to commemorate the love Mughal emperor of India, Shah Jahan, felt for his deceased wife, Mumtaz Mahal. In 1666, Shah Jahan also died and was buried next to his wife.

Taj Mahal

Over 1,000 elephants were used to haul marble to the site.

SECRETS OF STONE

The great pillars of Stonehenge rise from Salisbury Plain in southern England. The stones line up with the positions of the Sun and stars during the year. Stonehenge was probably a site for sacred rituals and was built in several stages between about 2600 and 1600 BC.

STONEHENGE

Some believe that Stonehenge was a calendar, a temple of the Sun, or a center of healing.

ANCIENT Empires

The great empires of the past once wielded immense power, governing vast areas and amassing great wealth. However, with their crumbling monuments all around, we are reminded that no power lasts forever—every empire must fall.

Defending the empire

Power attracts enemies, so empires need strong defenses. The Chinese emperors feared invasion by tribes who lived to the north. Between the 3rd century BC and the 16th century AD they built the world's longest network of fortifications—the Great Wall of China. The wall also served as an east-west route for trade and communications. Although impressive, the Great Wall failed to stop the Mongol invasion of China in the 1200s.

▲ Thousands of miles long, the original wall still stands in places, but some sections have been rebuilt in modern times.

IVORY QUEEN

Great empires often produced awesome works of art. This graceful head represents Queen Idia, the mother of Esigie who ruled the Benin Empire (in modern Nigeria) from 1504 to 1550. Many empires thrived in Africa before their lands were seized by European empire-builders in the 1800s and 1900s.

This ivory mask of Queen Idia is now at the Metropolitan Museum of Art, New York, U.S.

The King of Kings

The ruins of Persepolis still stand in southwest Iran. This was the city of Darius the Great, ruler of the Persian Empire from 522 to 486 BC. Persian lands eventually stretched from Western and Central Asia to Europe and North Africa. It was the biggest empire the world had ever known, ruling about 50 million people.

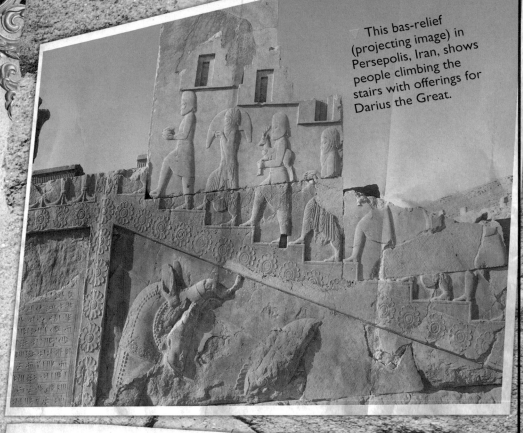

This bas-relief (projecting image) in Persepolis, Iran, shows people climbing the stairs with offerings for Darius the Great.

DURING THE MING DYNASTY (1368–1644), ONE MILLION SOLDIERS WERE STATIONED ALONG THE GREAT WALL OF CHINA.

Emperor of the Sun

An excited crowd gathers in an ancient Inca fortress at Cuzco, Peru, to watch a spectacular reenactment of the Sun festival of Inti Raymi. In the 1400s and early 1500s, the Inca Empire, called Tawantinsuyu, covered 2,403 mi (3,867 km) of South American coastal strip and mountains. The emperor, or Sapa Inca, was held in awe. He was believed to be a god, descended from the Sun. Each year he made sacrifices at the festival, which was held on June 24 (midwinter in the Southern Hemisphere).

▶ A modern presentation of the ancient Inca festival still impresses the crowds.

Power over peoples

Empires are many lands brought together under a single ruler or government. They depend not only on military power but also on administration, laws, and communications. These skills first came together in the Middle East. The world's very first empire was ruled by the city of Akkad, Mesopotamia, and was founded in 2334 BC by a ruler called Sharrum-Kin or Sargon I. It stretched from the Mediterranean Sea to the Persian Gulf, but had collapsed by about 2160 BC.

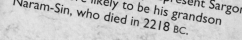

◀ This copper head may represent Sargon I, but it is more likely to be his grandson Naram-Sin, who died in 2218 BC.

51

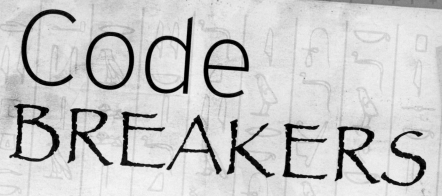

Code BREAKERS

If we are to travel back in history, we need to know the languages of the distant past. Often the words and scripts are long forgotten. They appear as strange symbols carved on rocks, tombs, or temples. Only language experts can solve these mysteries. Their work may take a lifetime, but if they succeed in cracking the code, they open up a window into the past.

The Rosetta riddle

In 1799 a slab of black stone was found at Rosetta (Rashid) in Egypt. It had been carved in three different scripts in 196 BC to mark the start of a ruler's reign. It was 1824 before all the words on the Rosetta Stone were correctly understood. The code was cracked by French genius Jean-François Champollion.

He started by matching known Greek letters on the third part with the Egyptian symbols on the first part. Then he counted and compared symbol frequency against other texts. The high number of ancient Egyptian hieroglyphs showed that they had to have several functions, representing sounds as well as objects and ideas.

▶ The Rosetta Stone has helped us to understand more about the amazing lives—and the even more amazing deaths—of the ancient Egyptians.

The top part was written in hieroglyphs, symbols that cover ancient Egyptian tombs and statues. No historian could work out what they meant.

The second part was written in Demotic, the everyday language of ancient Egypt. Another mystery.

The third part was written in ancient Greek, which people could understand. Finally, a key had been found to unlock the past.

ALLERS
FAMILJ-JOURNALEN
Pris: Helår 15: 50.
Allers Familj-Journals tryckeri-aktiebolag, Hälsingborg.
N:r 29.

Just som de ock vetenskapsmannen var i färd med att
här här, att han hade

Sir Henry to the rescue

In the 1830s and 40s, British scholar Sir Henry Rawlinson (1810–1895) became fascinated by carvings on Mount Behistun in Persia (modern Iran). The carvings were written in three ancient languages—Old Persian, Elamite, and Babylonian—and dated from the reign of King Darius the Great (548–486 BC). The inscriptions were written in cuneiform ("wedge-shaped") scripts. Rawlinson and others worked out that the Old Persian script represented sounds. They compared symbols and their frequency to work out the other two scripts.

◄ Rawlinson risked his life climbing a sheer rockface to get a closer look at the carvings.

History mystery

Great civilizations thrived in the cities of the Indus Valley (modern Pakistan) more than 4,500 years ago. Thousands of objects have been decorated with symbols, but no one knows what they mean. There are few of the repeats and combinations that normally make up a language, but computer tests carried out in 2009 suggest that this really was an ancient script.

► There are said to be about 417 symbols in the Indus script.

2011
1-VOLUME
IAN DICTIONARY
E UP OF 28,000
EIFORM WORDS—
UBLISHED BY THE
SITY OF CHICAGO.
OOK 90 YEARS TO
E AND THE WORK
ED 85 PEOPLE!

Back to the future

More than 3,000 years ago, Chinese fortune-tellers carved words onto animal bones and turtle shells, which they threw into a fire. As the bones cracked, the lines that appeared were believed to show glimpses of the future. These "oracle bone" scripts were ancestors of modern Chinese writing and provide historical information about the rulers of that period.

► When farmers dug up these bone fragments, thousands of years after they were carved, they thought they were magical dragon bones.

Some people believe that the Phaistos Disk is a forgery from 1908.

Secret spirals

The island of Crete, in southern Greece, has many ancient secrets, legends, and ruins. This clay disk was found at the ancient city of Phaistos and dates back to about 1700 BC. Its spirals of stamped designs have never been decoded. Some experts believe that a few of these symbols are similar to a mysterious Cretan script known as Linear A.

Out of the
ASHES

Although ancient people associated volcanic eruptions with angry gods, they often settled nearby because volcanic soil is rich and fertile—it was worth the risk. Volcanoes are symbols of nature's destructive powers, but they sometimes preserve the remains of humans and buildings. These sites are precious time capsules, where a moment in the past is frozen for eternity.

Mega-blast!

One of the most cataclysmic eruptions in history tore apart the Greek island of Thira, or Santorini, near Crete, perhaps in the 1620s BC. The sea rushed in and flooded the vast hole that was left behind. On the surviving land, a town was buried beneath a volcanic stone called pumice. Excavations at this site, named Akrotiri, began in 1967. They revealed drains, furniture, pottery, and stunning paintings in the Minoan style of ancient Crete.

▶ Footprints from the distant past, uncovered by Paul Abell, a member of Mary Leakey's team, in 1978. These hominids not only walked upright, but had feet very like our own.

Fossilized footprints

These footprints at Laetoli in Tanzania look as if they were made only yesterday. In fact, they are about 3.7 million years old and were made long before modern humans had evolved. They belong to hominids, the family of creatures that includes our distant ancestors. The marks were made in fine volcanic ash, which then set hard after being moistened by rain. The footprints became fossilized, preserved forever in stone.

The footprints are 7–8.5 in (18.5–21.5 cm) long.

The remains of Akrotiri reveal how the Minoan people lived more than 3,600 years ago.

▶ Plaster casts capture the moment at which people died in Pompeii.

Plastered!

The Italian city of Pompeii was buried under pumice and ash to a depth of up to 23 ft (7 m). Entire bodies became encased in the ash, leaving imprints as they decayed. Eventually only the skeletons remained. Archeologists discovered that by filling the cavities with plaster, they could recreate the citizens of Pompeii as they had appeared on that fateful day in AD 79.

POMPEII IN A FLASH

Imagine a whole city, stopped in its tracks in AD 79. Half-eaten meals are left on the table, dogs and people cower from the choking ash that showers down relentlessly. The city is entombed. Excavations at Pompeii have revealed the forum (marketplace), temples, streets, shops, houses, gardens, theaters, baths, taverns, laundries, and bakeries.

▶ This carbonized loaf of bread was found in an oven at Pompeii.

▶ This skeleton was excavated from the ruins of Herculaneum, with jeweled gold rings on its finger still intact.

Horrors in Herculaneum

Herculaneum was a small Italian seaside town just 4 mi (7 km) from Mount Vesuvius. The eruption of Vesuvius in AD 79 blasted it with ash and superhot water, burying the town under 50 ft (15 m) of boiling mud, which turned to rock. Many people fled before the disaster, but 300 or so were stranded in boathouses by the beach, trying to escape. Excavations since the 1700s have uncovered houses, public baths, fountains, jewelry, and wall paintings.

Can you imagine a modern city such as Sydney, Las Vegas, or Toronto being simply wiped off the map? How might such a site look to an archeologist in the future? Many thriving cities have been destroyed by floods, earthquakes, plague, or warfare. Sometimes climate change has turned fertile lands into deserts, which can no longer provide enough food to feed the city's inhabitants.

▶ Roots and tropical vines partially obscure the stonework of Angkor Wat.

Return of the wild

It takes no time at all for great monuments and cities to be reclaimed by nature. They become eroded by the wind, cracked by frost, or baked by the Sun. Roots and creepers take hold, covering, pushing, and concealing. In Cambodia, the awesome sites of Angkor Thom and the great temple of Angkor Wat, built in the 1100s to 1400s, would be swallowed up by tropical vegetation if they were not constantly cleared and maintained.

▶ Machu Picchu was built in about 1400 and abandoned after the Spanish invasion in 1532.

On the trail of the Incas

On steep mountain slopes in Peru there were mysterious traces of buildings and terraced fields, overgrown with trees and undergrowth. In 1911 an expedition led by the American archeologist Dr. Hiram Bingham (1875–1956) crossed the Urubamba River and climbed up toward the peak of Machu Picchu. Bingham began to clear the ruins and excavate. He discovered finely built stone houses, terraces, steep streets, temples, fountains, and workshops.

Sand and rock

Petra, in Jordan, was once the destination for camel caravans crossing the desert with their riches. The city was set in a cleft of rock and supplied with fresh water by aqueducts. Petra was the capital of the Nabataeans from the 500s BC and came under Roman rule in AD 106. Soon after, trade moved to coastal routes. The West didn't know of Petra's existence until 1812 when it was rediscovered by Johann Ludwig Burckhardt (1784–1817).

Petra's buildings were carved directly from the sandstone rockface.

THE MOAT THAT SURROUNDS THE TEMPLE OF ANGKOR WAT IS 4 MI (6 KM) LONG.

Early life

Çatalhöyük in Turkey was one of the world's earliest towns, settled between about 7500 and 5700 BC. Its houses were joined together, with no streets in between. This was a center of farming, crafts, and religious rituals. It may have been abandoned when trading patterns changed.

◀ This statue of the Mother Goddess was made in Çatalhöyük in about 6000 BC.

Discoveries of everyday items show historians how ordinary people lived their lives. We can relate these findings to our own lives to see how things have changed over the years.

Nordic chess piece
Isle of Lewis, Scotland
The Lewis chessmen were carved from walrus ivory, probably in Norway. All the pieces are human shapes, except the pawns.

1300s

Jar for scented oil
Makresia, Greece
Ancient Greeks kept cosmetics, ointments, scents, and oils in ornately decorated terra-cotta containers. Oils made their skin smooth and supple. Rich women also used face powder to achieve a fashionably pale complexion.

1700s

Maori comb
New Zealand
Maori men wore combs carved from whalebone or wood in their topknots (knot of hair arranged on the top of the head). The combs were regarded as sacred possessions.

Greek vase
Greece
Food and wine were stored in terra-cotta containers called amphorae. They kept goods cool.

Early 1900s

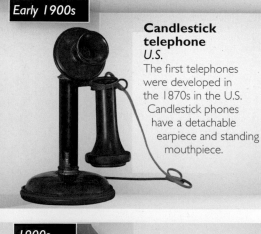

Candlestick telephone
U.S.
The first telephones were developed in the 1870s in the U.S. Candlestick phones have a detachable earpiece and standing mouthpiece.

EVERYDAY MEMORIES
The answers to questions about everyday life in the past are revealed by countless little clues. How did people dress and eat? Did they go to school? How did they make a living? How did they communicate with each other?

1900s

Phonograph
U.S.
Also called a gramophone, the phonograph could record and play music.

1400s

Aztec calendar stone
Mexico
This large stone shows details of months and historical ages.

c. 1150

Roman glassware
Rheims, France
Useful glassware was manufactured in many parts of the Roman Empire. These jugs and vases come from ancient Gaul.

C. AD 150

C. AD 1850

Victorian clothes
U.K.
A bonnet, shawl, calico skirt, jacket, and ankle boots were typical working-class clothes in the Victorian era.

5th–6th century

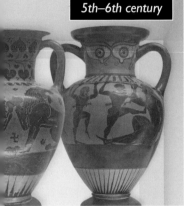

RELIVING THE PAST

Historical reenactments are organized to educate people about the past by making them feel like they are there. Museums and castles often recreate historical scenes by staging displays with actors and actresses. Even schoolchildren can dress up as Romans for the day to get an insight into what life was like in ancient Rome.

1950s

Television
U.S.
The Philco Predicta was a classic set from the early days of television.

50 BC–AD 50

Bronze mirror
Desborough, England
This elegant mirror decorated in the Celtic artistic style dates from Britain's Iron Age.

DRESSING UP
Many schoolchildren get the chance to dress up when they go to visit a museum or a historical building. For just one day they can feel like Victorians, or like a Norman family in a medieval castle.

AD 395–632

Wool balls, knitting needle, spool, and spindle
Coptic, Egypt
Ancient Egyptians knitted woolen socks. They had two tubes at the end for their toes, so they could be worn with sandals.

Land of the DEAD

F uneral rituals were already taking place tens of thousands of years ago. The way in which dead bodies have been treated has varied greatly over the ages and among different cultures and religions. The dead person might be buried, cremated, exposed in the open, or preserved as a mummy.

The puzzle of the "Red Lady"

In 1823, a skeleton was found in a cave at Paviland in Wales, U.K., by William Buckland (1784–1856). It was surrounded by shell jewelry and covered in a kind of red ocher. It was immediately assumed that this was the burial of a Roman lady. However, we now know that it was actually a young male who lived just over 29,000 years ago, perhaps the chief of a band of hunters.

The Paviland skeleton is the oldest known ceremonial burial in Western Europe.

Dou Wan's suit was made up of 2,156 plates of jade.

A gilded bronze oil lamp in the shape of a kneeling female servant, from the 2nd century BC, was found in the tomb of Princess Dou Wan.

The eternal princess

In China, princes and princesses were sometimes buried in beautiful suits made of small squares of jade bound by gold wire. This smooth, hard gemstone was believed to be magical, making the wearer immortal and preserving the body. Liu Sheng and his wife, Dou Wan, were buried in about 113 BC. Her tomb contained more than 3,000 precious items.

The grave robbers of Thebes

The trouble with filling the tombs of the dead with fabulous riches is that they attract thieves. To avoid this, the Egyptians began to bury their dead pharaohs in a secret necropolis (burial ground) in the cliffs near the city of Thebes (modern Luxor). Although the "Valley of the Kings," as it became known, was guarded day and night, robbers still managed to break into the tombs and steal the gold.

▲ Grave robbers risked their lives to steal the treasure of the pharaohs.

This statue of a ram from Ur is made of gold, silver, shell, and a blue stone called lapis lazuli.

The royal tombs of Ur

Ur was a city in Mesopotamia (ancient Iraq). Digs in the 1920s revealed 16 royal tombs dating from 2600 to 2500 BC. They were packed with treasure, including golden crowns, gaming boards, a lyre, and exquisite jewelry.

A funeral for a Viking

The Vikings were a seafaring people, so it is not surprising that they often chose to end their days at sea. The bodies of Viking chieftains might be burned in their boats, or gravestones might be laid out in the shape of a boat. This superb longship was found buried under an earthen mound at Oseberg in Norway. It contained the bodies of two women who died in AD 834. One of them may have been a queen.

The Oseberg ship contained dresses, veils, and other textiles, as well as finely carved chests, wooden sleighs, a cart, and the remains of horses, dogs, and an ox.

THE TOMBS OF UR ALSO INCLUDED DEATH PITS, WHERE MANY SERVANTS HAD BEEN SACRIFICED TO ACCOMPANY THE DEAD KINGS AND QUEENS TO THE NEXT WORLD.

Faces of

FOREVER

Some bodies are preserved naturally after death because of the conditions where they are buried. Others have been preserved on purpose for religious reasons, as some cultures believed it would allow the deceased to travel to the afterlife in one piece. The Egyptians perfected this skill.

▼ This mummy from Saqqara was discovered after 2,600 years.

In the land of deserts

Burials in desert sands can dry out dead bodies naturally. This is perhaps how the Egyptians first learned about mummification. They soon developed an elaborate process for preserving corpses artificially, using natron salt, cedar oil, resin, and bandages.

IN THE MIDDLE AGES, MUMMIES FROM RAIDED TOMBS WERE GROUND UP AND USED FOR MAKING MAGICAL POTIONS AND OINTMENTS.

Farewell, Artemidorus

When Egypt came under Greek and then Roman rule, dead bodies were still being mummified and buried in beautiful wooden coffins, which were shaped like human bodies. They were fitted with panels bearing very realistic portraits to provide a reminder of the deceased.

◄ This mummy case from Hawara shows the face of a young man called Artemidorus, who died about 1,900 years ago.

Towers of the dead

Mummification was common in the deserts and mountains of Chile and Peru from 5000 BC until the AD 1400s. In the plateaus of the high Andes, mummies were left in stone towers called chullpas, along with food, drink, knives, pots, and mirrors. In South America, mummies of children were sometimes placed in pottery urns and buried beneath the floor of the family home. Loving parents wanted them to be close at hand, where they could care for their spirit.

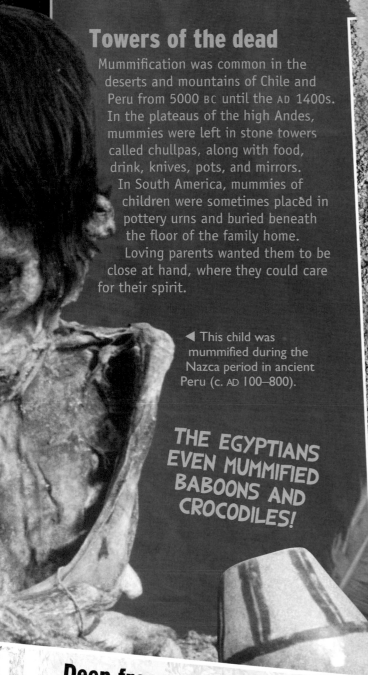

◀ This child was mummified during the Nazca period in ancient Peru (c. AD 100–800).

THE EGYPTIANS EVEN MUMMIFIED BABOONS AND CROCODILES!

THE BODIES IN THE BOG

The best-surviving bodies of all have been found in peaty wetlands. In the bogs of northern Europe, the cold, acidic conditions and a lack of oxygen have preserved the skin and organs. The bodies date from about 8000 BC to the early medieval period, but most are from the 5th to 1st century BC. Historians believe that they may have been violently killed as sacrifices to the gods.

A bog man from Lindow Moss, in England. He may have been sacrificed about 2,000 years ago.

Deep frozen

Ice has preserved corpses in the perpetually cold soil of Siberia, and in the mountain glaciers of Europe's Alps—just as if they have been kept in a natural freezer. In 1991 the body of a hunter from Europe's Copper Age was found on the border of Italy and Austria. It had been preserved in a glacier and was given the nickname of Ötzi the Iceman.

▲ The Iceman is the oldest complete human mummy ever to be found. He is so well preserved, even his eyes are still visible.

VISAS

Name: Ötzi

Date of birth: c. 3300 BC

Place of Residence: The Alps, Europe

Age at time of death: c. 45 years

Height: 5ft 5 in (1.65 m)

Weight: 110 lb (50 kg)

Distinguishing marks: Tattoos (or needle treatment)

Dress: Bearskin cap, cloak, leather coat, belt, leggings, and shoes

Possessions: Flint knife, bow and arrows, copper ax

HISTORY Lab

S cience and technology have transformed the work of historians and archeologists. Special techniques can be used to determine what people ate just before they died, the cause of death, and even what type of work they did. They even reveal what the climate and plant life were like thousands of years ago.

As a tree grows it produces more layers of cells, or rings, in its trunk. These can provide clues about past climates.

It's all in the trunk

Dendrochronology is the scientific term for counting the annual growth rings in wood. The number of rings offers an accurate year count. The width of the rings provides information about climate and growing conditions.

Genetic tools

DNA is the chemical code of inheritance in all living things and genetics is now a vital tool in archeology. As well as helping to identify a mummy, DNA analysis can also give historians a greater understanding of the time in which the person lived. Diseases the mummy suffered from and medicines it took, as well as its family lineage can also be discovered.

DNA tests suggest that this is the mummy of Hatshepsut, an Egyptian queen who ruled as pharaoh in the 15th century BC.

A sample for carbon dating is taken from a reindeer bone.

Radioactive material

Elements that break down naturally give out radiation. They are said be "radioactive." Organic remains such as wood, grain, textiles, or bones contain both radioactive carbon-14 atoms and stable carbon-12 atoms, which can be compared. The older the object, the less radioactive it will be.

A microscopic triumph

An electron microscope was used to study three tiny grains of pollen found in the stomach of the mummy Ötzi the Iceman. This gave archeologists information about where and when Ötzi died, including the local climate and vegetation, and the season. Electron microscopes were also used to identify food particles in his gut.

▶ Ötzi's last breakfast had been a type of wheat, probably made into a coarse bread.

Call in the dentist

Teeth are the █████est, toughest part of the human body. They often survive long after the bones have rotted away. By studying just one tooth and its wear and tear, it is possible to build up a picture of a person's life. Age, diet, methods of food preparation, general health, stress levels, hygiene, evidence of famine, and lines of descent can all be revealed.

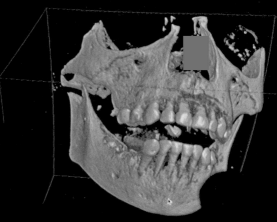

▲ A CT (computer tomography) scan is used to create digital models of a child's jaw and teeth from its 2,000-year-old mummy.

Scans and X-rays

In hospitals, patients can be examined using X-rays and a variety of other scanning technology. This equipment is perfect for examining fragile mummies or other remains. Even removing the delicate bandaging of a mummy can be disastrous, but an X-ray can see straight through to the bone or the skull without causing damage.

This naturally mummified body dates from the 1700s and was taken from a church crypt in Hungary. Scans showed that the cause of death was tuberculosis.

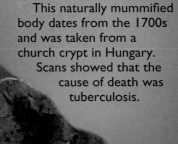

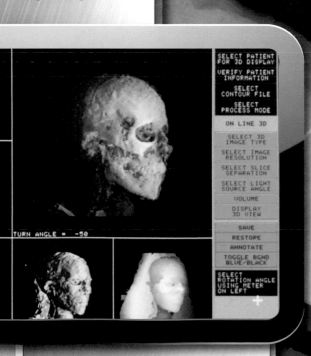

▲ These scans were taken through the closed coffin of an Egyptian temple singer who lived in about 950 BC.

Treasure Trove

Finds of treasure involve fabulous wealth, precious objects, dazzling beauty, and tales of greed and robbery. Valuable discoveries can inform historians about past societies. They learn how things were made and what was considered to be valuable.

HIDDEN HOARDS

Treasure was often hidden in secret places. People may have been smuggling stolen loot, hiding their riches from an invading army, or safely "banking" their money. If the owners were killed or forced to flee before they could reclaim their hoard, its whereabouts may be lost for centuries.

▲ A Viking treasure hoard from about AD 860, found at Hon, in Norway.

▲ The Crusaders shipped the bronze horses back to Venice, Italy, where they became one of the city's most famous sights.

THE SACKING OF A CITY

In 1204, a Christian army of Venetian and French Crusaders bound for the Middle East turned aside to launch a brutal attack on the Christian city of Constantinople (modern Istanbul). They sacked the great churches and palaces, stealing silver, gold, precious stones, pearls, silk textiles, and sacred relics. They carried off a vast fortune and even stole the magnificent statues of horses from the city's racetrack.

FROM THE TOMBS OF LORDS

Many of the most dazzling treasures from all over the world have been found in the tombs and graves of royalty or high-ranking nobles. Grave goods may have been intended as objects for the dead to take to the afterlife, or they may be items of religious ritual or badges of rank.

◄ The Moche "Lord" of Sipán, who lived in Peru about 1,800 years ago, was buried in a pyramid along with gold, silver, and 400 jewels.

CROWN JEWELS

Kings, queens, and emperors liked to display their status and wealth with ceremonial treasures, called regalia, that they wore or carried. Often made of gold or covered in jewels, they included crowns, tiaras, diadems, chains, swords, rings, gloves, orbs (globes), scepters (ornamental staffs), and ermine-trimmed cloaks. Historical crown jewels—or duplicates—are often put on display.

GIFTS FOR THE GODS

◄ The Guarrazar treasure contained crowns, sapphires, and pearls. It was given to the Church in the 600s AD, by Germanic kings who ruled in Spain.

People have always made offerings to their spirits or gods, such as incense, sacrifices, or food. "Votive" offerings may also have included fine weapons or jewelry, thrown into a sacred pool or left at a shrine. Medieval rulers would try to win divine favor by giving rich treasures to temples, monasteries, or churches.

▲ This crown, orb, and scepter were owned by the kings of Poland.

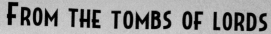

ABOUT 3,000 OF THE OLDEST GOLD ITEMS WERE FOUND IN VARNA, BULGARIA, DATING FROM 4700–4200 BC.

Return to the BATTLEFIELD

Wartime memorabilia, eyewitness accounts, and historical records help archeologists to build a picture of the realities of wartime. Sometimes their research can reveal forgotten stories, correct inaccurate records, or add significant material to historical archives.

Army maps of the time help archeologists and historians locate battlefield sites, tunnels, and trenches. Archeologists are then able to produce modern maps based on their discoveries.

Boesinghe
Elverdinghe
Brielen
Bryke
Vlamertinghe
YPRES
Dickebusch
Kuisstraathoek
Plas
Voorm
Wyts

French line
Canadian line
British line
Central Division (British)
Cavalry Corps which took the place of the Central Division on May 13
"A" Division (British; originally Colonel Geddes' mixed brigade)

Fading photographs

Traveling back to World War I (1914–1918) is made easier by the widespread use of photography at that time. We can see the expressions on the faces of the young men on both sides as they marched to the front line, lived in the mud of the trenches, and went into battle—history as it actually happened.

▶ Albert "Smiler" Marshall (on horseback) survived World War I and lived until 2005.

In World War I, the Belgian city of Ypres was destroyed during repeated battles.

Letters and diaries

The authentic voices of World War I soldiers have survived in their diaries and in the letters sent home from the front line, even those that were censored for security reasons by the military authorities.

English Miles

Shaded area indicates ground won by Germans as a result of the first great gas attack.

Digging into history

Both sides fighting in World War I (the Allies and the Central Powers) dug networks of trenches to protect their troops, from the North Sea to Switzerland. Archeologists in the Somme region of France dig the battlefield sites to discover the exact position of the trenches of 1916. Archeological finds include skeletons, uniform buttons and badges, helmets, and the remains of weapons, bullets, and shells.

▶ British author Michael Morpurgo visits the Flanders Field Museum in Ypres.

Remains of soldiers who fell during the horrific battles of 1916 are still being uncovered today.

MUSEUMS TELL THE STORY

War was a confusing and terrifying experience for many of the troops on the ground. They could not know the bigger picture of World War I as it progressed. Today, historians can research the tactics and strategies of the generals and the everyday life of the troops by visiting museums and battlefields.

Remembering the soldiers

Cemeteries and memorials are found all over the battlefields of World War I. The huge scale of these burial grounds is a sobering sight. The graves are still visited by descendants of the soldiers who died, and they also provide useful information for war historians.

▲ The names of over 54,000 missing soldiers are recorded on the Menin Gate Memorial in Ypres.

OCEAN Depths

Another world exists beneath the waves. Amid sandbanks and coral reefs, marine archeologists search for the remains of ancient shipwrecks—the victims of storms or naval battles long ago. These are precious time capsules, but are often difficult to access in deep, dangerous waters.

Titanic!

"Titanic" means gigantic, and this was the name given to a state-of-the-art, trans-Atlantic, luxury liner a century ago. In 1912, on its maiden voyage, the ship struck an iceberg and went down with the loss of more than 1,500 lives. It became the most famous shipwreck of all time. In 1985, the remains of *Titanic* were discovered at a depth of nearly 2.5 mi (4 km). More than 6,000 items, including plates and the ship's whistle, have been recovered.

A submersible's camera reveals the rails of the *Titanic*.

Classical cargo

The ancient Greeks were great seafarers and colonists, trading all over the Mediterranean Sea and the Black Sea from the 9th century BC. Wrecks reveal shipbuilding and navigation methods, while surviving cargoes tell us about trading patterns, economics, and even Greek art. Finds include amphorae, the large pottery jars used to store wine and oil.

This is the world's earliest known mechanical computer, dating back to about 100 BC. It was discovered in a Greek shipwreck.

▼ The *Mary Rose* is raised from the seabed in a giant mechanical cradle.

The lost warship

Back in 1545, the warship *Mary Rose* was the pride of the English navy and of King Henry VIII. She was fitted with new "gun ports," openings in the ship's side that allowed the firing of heavy cannon. Sailing out to meet the French fleet, *Mary Rose* flooded and sank. The wreck was found in 1971, many of its timbers preserved under the seabed.

Treasure galleons

After Spanish soldiers invaded Central and South America in the 1500s, they shipped a fortune in looted treasure back to Spain. Between 1566 and 1789, they organized convoys of big sailing ships called galleons to set out from the Caribbean Sea across the Atlantic Ocean. Many ships in these treasure fleets were attacked by pirates, or sunk by hurricanes. The *Nuestra Señora de Atocha* was part of a fleet wrecked on coral reefs off Florida, U.S., in 1622. This ship, with its precious cargo, coins, and cannon, was found in 1985 by American treasure hunters.

IN 1967, DIVERS LOCATED A GREEK CITY THAT SANK BENEATH THE WAVES ABOUT 3,000 YEARS AGO. REMAINS FROM THE PAVLOPETRI SITE HAVE BEEN DATED TO BETWEEN 2800 AND 1200 BC.

▶ This ring and Spanish coin were salvaged from the wreck of a pirate ship, the *Whydah*, which sank off Cape Cod, in North America, in 1717.

Air to GROUND

Archeologists have found the most awesome historical sites—from the air! Images of Earth from air or space can reveal ancient patterns of fields, settlements, or earthworks that could never be seen from the ground. These show the whole of a historic site in its landscape, revealing its overall layout and features.

▼ A microlight aircraft flies over the landscape of Wiltshire in England, which is world famous for its prehistoric monuments.

In the early Middle Ages, Avebury village was built across part of the henge.

High above Avebury

From the ground, the site of Avebury, Wiltshire, U.K., is impressive. From the air, it makes sense. Earthworks form a great ring containing three circles of standing stones. This "henge" was raised from about 2850 BC to 2200 BC, during the New Stone Age. Archeologists believe that it was originally used for ceremonies or rituals.

Stonehenge revealed

The plan of Stonehenge becomes very clear from the air. The position of the great stones and the outer earthworks is emphasized by light and shadow. The site is part of a much larger sacred and ceremonial landscape.

◀ A view never seen during the first 4,900 years of Stonehenge's existence.

Monkey puzzle

Scratched out of the soil in Peru's Nazca Desert are huge patterns and pictures of birds, animals, and people. It was not until the invention of aircraft that people could really see these for what they were. They date back to AD 400–650 and may represent messages to the gods or ceremonial pathways.

SOME OF THE NAZCA DRAWINGS ARE AN ENORMOUS 660 FT (200 M) ACROSS!

▲ This Nazca Desert drawing shows a gigantic monkey with a curly tail.

► Found in Ohio, U.S., the first recorded sightings of the Great Serpent Mound are from the 1800s.

Snaking through the landscape

The Great Serpent Mound is the largest animal-shaped mound, or effigy, in the world, at 1,348 ft (411 m) long and up to 3 ft (one meter) high. It is believed to have been built by the Native Americans in AD 1070. After excavating the site, researchers now believe that it was not a burial site.

Rebuilding HISTORY

History can easily be destroyed or lost. Wood rots, stone and brick crumble, costumes deteriorate, written records are easily torn, and precious metals may be stolen and melted down. Saving and recovering the evidence of history is crucial—using conservation, restoration, and reconstruction.

BEFORE

AFTER

Shards of pottery may be carefully reassembled and stuck together.

Jigsaw puzzles

Imagine a vase shattered into a thousand fragments, or an ancient scroll that has disintegrated into a handful of scraps. Often all that remains of a helmet, shield, or bowl are a few crumbling strips of bronze. Experts spend many hours putting together the pieces of the jigsaw, from which pieces may be missing. Sometimes it is not known what the object is until the puzzle is completed.

A painting by Guido Reni (1575–1642) is carefully restored.

BEFORE

AFTER

Canvas and paint

Restoring precious paintings requires painstaking care. Removing centuries of grime or varnish may reveal the colors in startling freshness, or even cast doubt on who painted the picture in the first place. X-rays may reveal corrections the artist has made while painting, or changes that others have made later. Pigments or canvas repairs must be carefully matched with the originals.

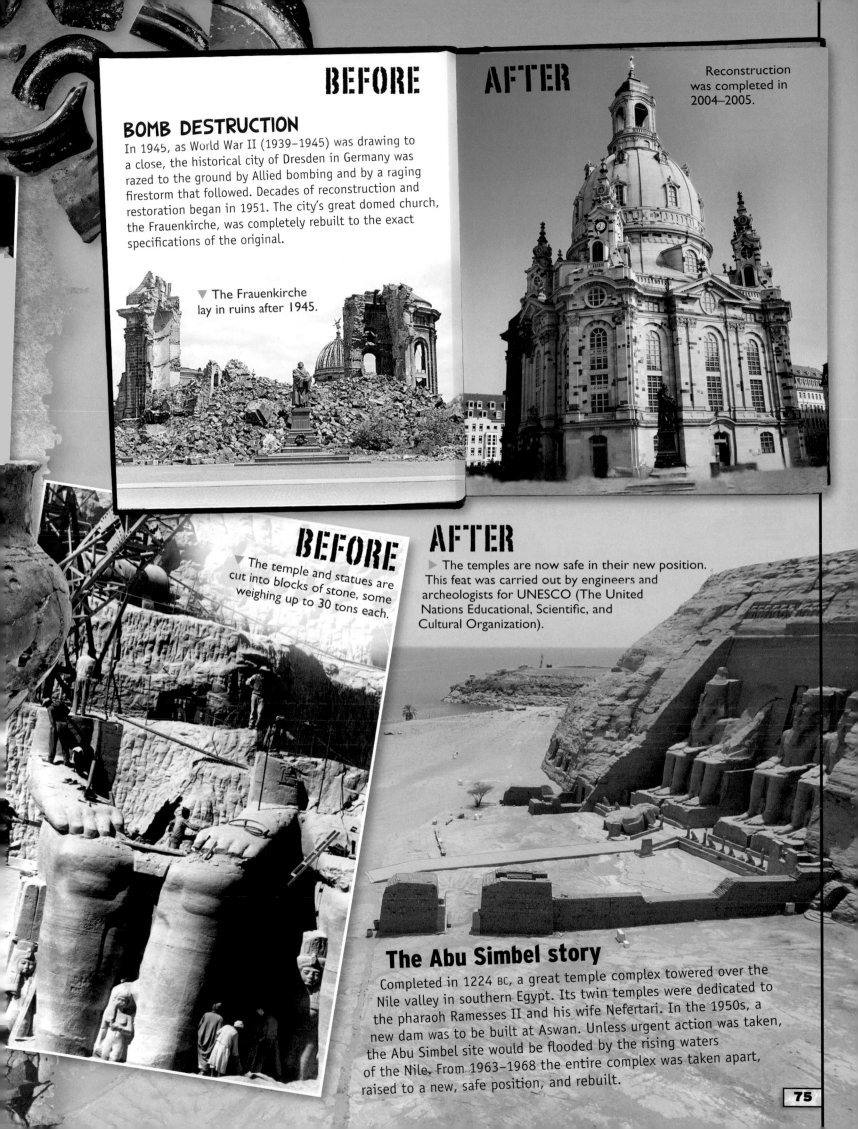

BEFORE

BOMB DESTRUCTION

In 1945, as World War II (1939–1945) was drawing to a close, the historical city of Dresden in Germany was razed to the ground by Allied bombing and by a raging firestorm that followed. Decades of reconstruction and restoration began in 1951. The city's great domed church, the Frauenkirche, was completely rebuilt to the exact specifications of the original.

▼ The Frauenkirche lay in ruins after 1945.

AFTER

Reconstruction was completed in 2004–2005.

BEFORE

▼ The temple and statues are cut into blocks of stone, some weighing up to 30 tons each.

AFTER

▶ The temples are now safe in their new position. This feat was carried out by engineers and archeologists for UNESCO (The United Nations Educational, Scientific, and Cultural Organization).

The Abu Simbel story

Completed in 1224 BC, a great temple complex towered over the Nile valley in southern Egypt. Its twin temples were dedicated to the pharaoh Ramesses II and his wife Nefertari. In the 1950s, a new dam was to be built at Aswan. Unless urgent action was taken, the Abu Simbel site would be flooded by the rising waters of the Nile. From 1963–1968 the entire complex was taken apart, raised to a new, safe position, and rebuilt.

TEMPLES OF TIME

We can't all visit lost cities or discover treasure, but we can go to local historical sites, museums, and galleries. They act as centers of education, research, conservation, and debate. Curators and archivists recreate scenes from the past using real objects and showcase awesome artifacts used by people, hundreds or thousands of years ago.

▶ See the record-breaking American plane *Spirit of St. Louis* (1927) at Washington's National Air and Space Museum.

Get inspired

Designers can get their inspiration from the many fashions of the past. Many museums around the world have stunning displays of historic dress, stage costumes, and fine jewelry.

▲ Fine tapestries from France's National Museum of the Middle Ages, in Paris.

Treasures from around the world

Some of the most famous museums are the Louvre in Paris, France, the Metropolitan Museum of Art in New York City, U.S., the British Museum in London, U.K., and the Smithsonian Museums (19 are located in Washington D.C., U.S.). Exhibits full of historical treasures may be seen from all over the world. Although exciting for visitors, this can be a matter of international dispute as some people believe that treasures should be returned to their homeland.

▲ A ballgown worn by Queen Victoria in 1851 was shown at the Queen's Gallery of Buckingham Palace in London, U.K.

All at sea

Barcelona's medieval royal shipyard is the historic setting for a splendid maritime museum packed with historical ships from ornate galleys to fishing boats. Like many museums it tells you much more besides—about mapping and navigation, political history, trade, and economics.

▼ A replica of the 1568 Royal Galley of Don John of Austria.

Totem poles

Museums of anthropology introduce us to human societies and cultures of the past. This totem pole, made by the Haida people, is from the collection at the University of British Columbia, in Canada. In the 1800s, tall wooden carvings were symbols of power, prestige, and family groups.

◀ Ethnic carvings from long ago still inspire many modern artists and sculptors.

▲ Ancient Babylon's Processional Way (c. 575 BC) is recreated at the Pergamon Museum in Berlin, Germany.

Building HISTORY

Spectacular structures reveal our past—explore a world of colossal constructions from mighty prehistoric monuments to luxurious royal residences.

◄ Athens, the greatest city in ancient Greece, is home to the magnificent Parthenon temple. This imposing structure was built between 447 BC and 432 BC and housed a 50-ft- (15-m-) high gold-and-marble statue of Athena, the city's guardian goddess.

Mighty MEGALITHS

Dotted across western Europe are large numbers of ancient earth monuments and standing stones, known as megaliths. Some of these spectacular structures date back to the Stone Age, around 5,000 years ago. The people who built them had few tools, yet they still managed to haul the huge stones vast distances. We don't know for sure why they were built, but they may have had a ceremonial or religious significance.

▼ Work began erecting Stonehenge around 2600 BC, and continued for more than 1,000 years.

Staggering Stonehenge

One of the most impressive monuments in the world, Stonehenge stands proudly in the middle of Salisbury Plain, U.K. Today, this mysterious structure consists of a central horseshoe of 43 standing stones surrounded by a larger circle of 30 standing stones, which has a ring of flat stones laid on top. Some are enormous—up to 13.5 ft (4.1 m) tall and weighing around 25 tons (22.7 tonnes). They may have been dragged all the way from the Preseli Hills in South Wales, 150 mi (241 km) away.

Shrouded in mystery

There are many theories about the purpose of Stonehenge. It might have been a temple to the gods or a monument to the dead. It might also have been a symbol of unity between the warring tribes of England, as large numbers of different people would have had to work together to build it. Recently, it has been suggested that it was a vast healing site. The Preseli stones came from near a natural spring, so it is possible that people came to Stonehenge hoping to be cured of their illnesses.

▲ Stonehenge has long been a center of religious importance. Throughout its history, groups such as Druids have gathered there to celebrate the seasons.

50,000 PIECES OF BONE FROM 63 MEN, WOMEN, AND CHILDREN HAVE BEEN FOUND BURIED NEAR STONEHENGE. THEIR IDENTITIES ARE A MYSTERY.

▶ It is probable that Newgrange, a vast burial mound, held some major religious significance related to the winter sun.

Ancient passage tomb

Five hundred years older than Stonehenge and the pyramids of Egypt, Newgrange Mound in Ireland is the oldest surviving architectural masterpiece in the world. This enormous circular mound was built of layers of stone and earth in around 3200 BC. It is 39 ft (12 m) tall, 249 ft (76 m) wide, and covers an enormous area of 48,437 sq ft (4,500 sq m).

INSIDE THE MOUND

In the southeast of the mound, a passage less than 66 ft (20 m) long leads into a cross-shaped burial chamber. The 20-ft- (6-m-) high stone roof has kept this area dry for more than 5,000 years. At 8.58 a.m. on December 21—the winter solstice or shortest day of the year—a narrow beam of sunlight shines down the passage and hits a triple-spiral design carved on the wall.

▼ These diagrams show two different views of how, once a year, a narrow beam of sunlight enters the mound and lights up the end wall.

Side view

Roof box

Entrance stone

Path of winter solstice sunlight

Stone basin

Passage

Burial chamber

Kerb stones

Overhead view

▼ Scotsman James Miln and his French assistant, a boy named Zacharie Le Rouzic, first began to count the Carnac stones in the 1860s.

Row upon row

The standing stones at Carnac, France, are nothing short of impressive. Eleven rows of 1,100 menhirs, or prehistoric standing stones, some a huge 13 ft (4 m) tall, stretch for 3,822 ft (1,165 m). Not far away are another ten rows of 1,029 stones, which run for around 4,265 ft (1,300 m). Close by are a smaller group of 555 stones, as well as several tumuli (grave mounds) and dolmens (free-standing graves). In total, this village has more than 3,000 stones, all erected around 3300 BC by the local Stone Age people. They may have been used to detect earthquakes, which were common in this area.

PYRAMID Power

Standing in the Egyptian desert to the west of Cairo is the Great Pyramid. It was the tallest man-made structure in the world for more than 3,800 years, built to house the body of the pharaoh after his death. Thousands of workers toiled under a blazing sun for 20 years to build this colossal structure.

A symbol of power

The Great Pyramid is the largest and the oldest of the three pyramids at Giza. It was built for the Pharaoh Khufu, who ruled Egypt between 2585 and 2560 BC. He wanted a tomb more grand and impressive than any pharaoh before him. The pyramid was once 480 ft (146.3 m) tall, although it has eroded over the years to become 455 ft (139 m) in height. Incredibly, the pyramid contains roughly 2.3 million limestone blocks. Since it took 20 years to build, it is estimated that workers would have had to place 12 blocks each hour, a total of 896 tons (812 tonnes) of stone a day.

Building the tomb

The thousands of workers that built the Great Pyramid were directed by a man called Hemiunu, whose job title was "Overseer of All the King's Works." He decided where to build the enormous structure, and how to do so. Hemiunu organized every aspect of the mammoth project, from the quarrying of the stone to the preparation of houses for the laborers. We don't know for certain how the workers moved the stones up the sides of the pyramid, but it is likely that they dragged or rolled them up a ramp with ropes, rollers—and hard labor.

▲ Each block used to build the Great Pyramid weighed as much as two and a half adult elephants.

▼ The Great Pyramid was once coated with blocks of highly polished white limestone, but these have since been removed to build mosques and other buildings in Cairo.

▶ The Great Sphinx is 241 ft (73.5 m) long, 63 ft (19 m) wide, and 66 ft (20 m tall).

STAIRWAY TO THE SUN

The pyramids were associated with the Egyptian Sun god Ra, who was usually shown with the head of a falcon and a sun-disk resting on his head. The Egyptians believed that when a pharaoh died, the Sun would strengthen its beams to create a heavenly ramp or stairway, which the pharaoh's soul would ascend to the heavens. A pyramid represented this ramp on earth.

A colossal guardian

Sitting guard by the three pyramids at Giza is the Great Sphinx. It was carved out of solid rock, and has the body of a lion and the head, probably, of Pharaoh Khafre, whose pyramid is next to Khufu's. The ancient Egyptians considered lions to be guardians, so this massive statue was probably built to protect the pyramids.

▲ The Step Pyramid was once surrounded by courtyards and ceremonial buildings. It measures 203 ft (62 m) in height.

Changes in design

The first pyramid to be built was for Pharaoh Djoser. It was completed by 2611 BC, and consists of six mastabas (platforms) of decreasing size placed on top of each other. The steps were believed to serve as a giant stairway for the pharaoh to reach the heavens. Later pyramids, like the ones at Giza, have flat sides. Most of these tombs were built for pharaohs during the periods of Egyptian history known as the Old and Middle Kingdoms, from 2585 to 1814 BC.

AWESOME Landmarks

Cities are known for their landmarks—recognizable buildings or structures with historical significance. Some are enormous palaces and temples, others imposing gates or high towers. The most impressive monuments attract travelers, who come to marvel at the feats of construction or to learn about their place in history.

WORLD GUIDES

SPAIN

THE PARTHENON

The Parthenon, an ancient Greek temple, stands on the Acropolis (a rocky hilltop) in the center of Athens, the capital of Greece. It is dedicated to the goddess Athena, and was completed by 438 BC. Measuring 228 ft (69.5 m) by 101 ft (31 m), the temple is surrounded by stone columns, and it once had a gently sloping roof. It has had many uses over time—a treasury, a Christian church, and a Muslim mosque.

GREECE

THE ALHAMBRA

Set on a wooded hill in the south of Spain, the Alhambra is arguably one of the finest palaces in the world. Originally built as a fortress in AD 889, it was later converted to a sumptuous palace by Yusuf I, Muslim Sultan of Granada, in 1333. Inside the palace walls are beautifully decorated rooms and halls, with splendid gardens, fountains, and pools to keep the palace cool in summer.

WORLD GUIDES

USA

ALCATRAZ ISLAND

Off the coast of San Francisco in California, U.S., lies an infamous landmark—Alcatraz Island. Now popular with tourists, it was once a prison, home to some of the most violent criminals in America. The cold, treacherous waters that separate the island from the coast made it incredibly isolated and—importantly—highly difficult to escape.

THE BRANDENBURG GATE

Standing in the center of Berlin, Germany, is the mighty Brandenburg Gate. Opened in 1791, this structure is 66 ft (20 m) tall, 213 ft (65 m) wide, and 36 ft (11 m) deep. Incredibly, it survived bombing during World War II (1939–1945). After 1961 it formed part of the Berlin Wall, which divided the city of Berlin into eastern and western sections. The wall came down in 1989 and today it is a symbol of the reunited city.

BIG BEN

The tower attached to the Houses of Parliament in London, U.K., is known as Big Ben—but this is not its real name. It was originally called the Clock Tower, before being renamed Elizabeth Tower in 2012. Big Ben is actually the great bell inside the tower. Its greatest claim to fame, other than its world-famous chimes, is that it holds the largest four-faced, chiming clock in the world.

THE EIFFEL TOWER

In 1889, The World's Fair—an international exhibition—was staged in Paris, France. The Eiffel Tower, a tall iron arch, was built to impress the many visitors to the city. This vast structure remained the tallest building in the world for 41 years, until the Chrysler Building in New York, U.S., was built in 1930. In 1957, the Eiffel grew by 17 ft (5.2 m) to its present height—1,063-ft- (324-m-) high—when an antenna was added to its top.

THE FORBIDDEN CITY

Inside Beijing, China, is a vast complex known as the Forbidden City. It used to be the imperial palace, home to the emperor and his family. Built between 1406 and 1420, it contains 980 buildings and covers more than 7,750,000 sq ft (720,000 sq m). More than one million workers built the many courtyards, temples, palaces, and bridges.

City of STONE

Hidden in the red sandstone hills of Jordan is the beautiful city of Petra. Carved out of the solid rock are palaces, temples, churches, streets full of houses and stores, theaters, and tombs. The city was built by the Nabataeans, a wealthy tribe that traded across the desert region, from the 1st century BC. They built Petra as their capital, damming local streams to create a constant source of water.

The tombs

There are hundreds of tombs carved into the solid rock. Many of them have elaborately carved fronts with pillars, arches, and other architectural features to make them look like real buildings. Some tombs are enormous—construction would have been a huge task.

▼ The Palace Tomb is one of the largest monuments in Petra.

An ancient theater

The stone theater is of Roman design, with 33 rows of seats cut into the solid rock. The seats face the remains of a stage and dressing rooms. Unfortunately it is not known what sort of plays would have been performed here.

Enter the city

The main entrance to Petra is through a narrow gorge known as the Siq ("the shaft"). The passageway is a natural fault that winds for 0.75 mi (1.2 km) between the sandstone hills that tower 590 ft (180 m) above it. In some places the Siq is only 10–13 ft (3–4 m) wide. Traders entered the city through the Siq, bringing silks, spices, and other riches from across the East to trade and barter.

▼ The theater is in the shape of a semicircle. It is one of the city's most notable structures.

▶ On top of Al Khazneh are four stone eagles. The Nabataeans believed that they carried away the souls of the dead people buried inside.

Beautiful building

Al Khazneh—one of the most beautiful buildings in Petra—was built as a mausoleum for the dead. Its Arabic name means "the Treasury," as one legend says that local bandits hid their loot in the stone urn high up on the front of the building. As the urn is solid sandstone, this would not have been possible.

▲ Visitors to Petra can still walk through the Siq—the long, twisting passageway that leads to the ancient city.

Great Wall

Stretching across the northern plains and hills of China are a series of remarkable fortifications. They are collectively known as the Great Wall of China. Some are built of stone, many more are mounds of earth. Others are just ditches or natural frontiers, such as cliffs and rivers. Together, they form one of the greatest architectural wonders of the world.

The need for defense

China was often threated by hostile tribes living to its north. To protect themselves, the various Chinese states built a series of local walls. When China was united under the First Emperor in 221 BC, these walls were joined together. Parts of this new wall were built of stone, while other parts were constructed with earth. This wall was then extended, and large parts were rebuilt in stone and brick. It is these latest walls that we recognize today as the Great Wall.

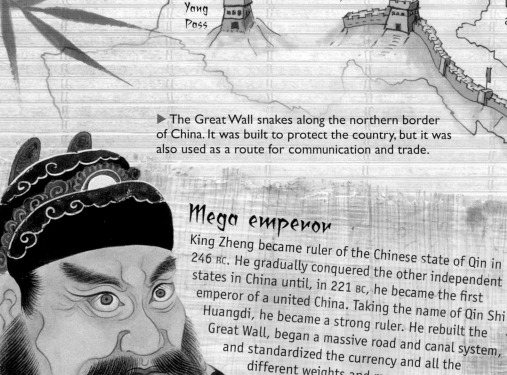

Yang Pass

Jiayu Pass

Ningxia Pass

▶ The Great Wall snakes along the northern border of China. It was built to protect the country, but it was also used as a route for communication and trade.

Mega emperor

King Zheng became ruler of the Chinese state of Qin in 246 BC. He gradually conquered the other independent states in China until, in 221 BC, he became the first emperor of a united China. Taking the name of Qin Shi Huangdi, he became a strong ruler. He rebuilt the Great Wall, began a massive road and canal system, and standardized the currency and all the different weights and measures. When he died in 210 BC, he was buried alongside a vast army of terra-cotta warriors to guard him in the afterlife.

◀ The First Emperor was a strong but cruel ruler. He once ordered 460 scholars to be buried alive for owning forbidden books.

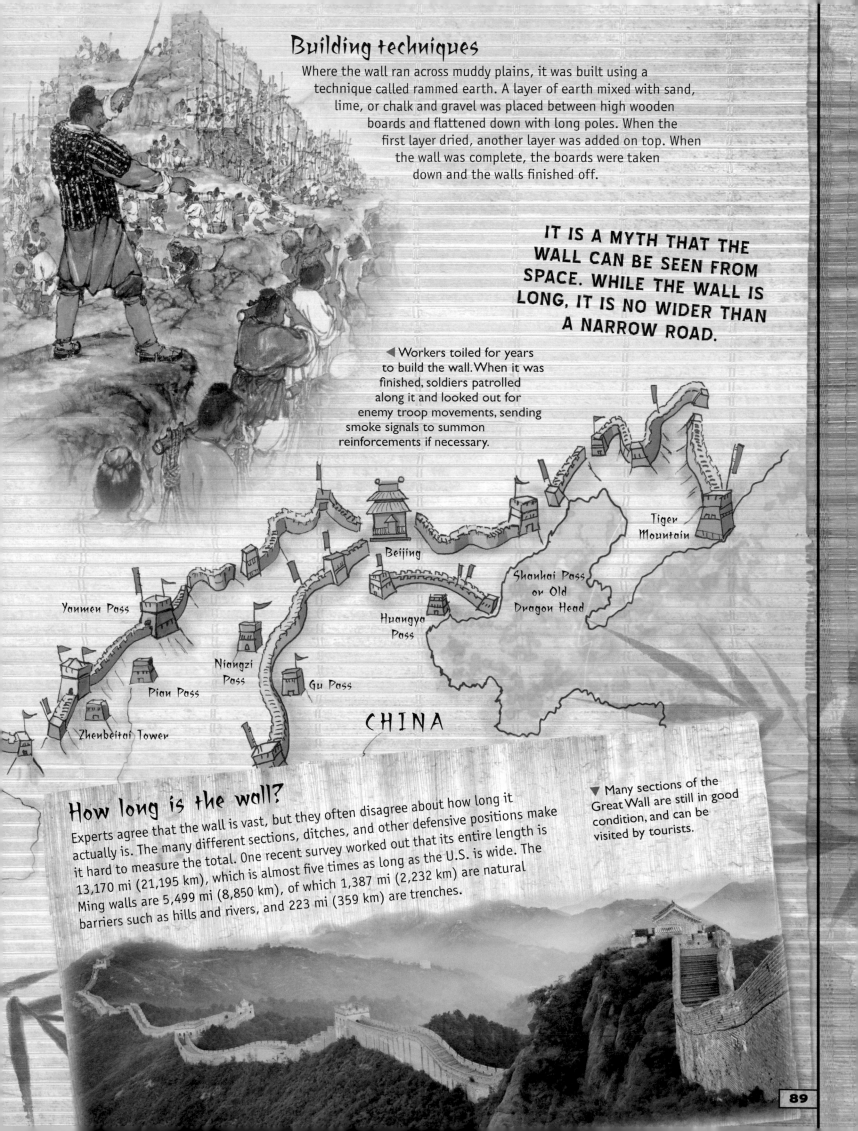

Building techniques

Where the wall ran across muddy plains, it was built using a technique called rammed earth. A layer of earth mixed with sand, lime, or chalk and gravel was placed between high wooden boards and flattened down with long poles. When the first layer dried, another layer was added on top. When the wall was complete, the boards were taken down and the walls finished off.

IT IS A MYTH THAT THE WALL CAN BE SEEN FROM SPACE. WHILE THE WALL IS LONG, IT IS NO WIDER THAN A NARROW ROAD.

◀ Workers toiled for years to build the wall. When it was finished, soldiers patrolled along it and looked out for enemy troop movements, sending smoke signals to summon reinforcements if necessary.

Yanmen Pass

Beijing

Tiger Mountain

Shanhai Pass or Old Dragon Head

Huangya Pass

Niangzi Pass

Pian Pass

Gu Pass

Zhenbeitai Tower

CHINA

How long is the wall?

Experts agree that the wall is vast, but they often disagree about how long it actually is. The many different sections, ditches, and other defensive positions make it hard to measure the total. One recent survey worked out that its entire length is 13,170 mi (21,195 km), which is almost five times as long as the U.S. is wide. The Ming walls are 5,499 mi (8,850 km), of which 1,387 mi (2,232 km) are natural barriers such as hills and rivers, and 223 mi (359 km) are trenches.

▼ Many sections of the Great Wall are still in good condition, and can be visited by tourists.

BRIDGING the World

Throughout history people have needed to cross over and manage waterways—this has resulted in the assembly of some impressive bridges. Many are awesome because of their size, others for their ingenuity in design and construction, and some for their sheer beauty.

BRIDGE OF SIGHS, ITALY

This famous bridge was built over a narrow canal in Venice in 1602, and is entirely enclosed in white marble. On one side were rooms in the chief magistrate's palace, where criminals were questioned. If found guilty, the convicts were led across to the New Prison. On their way, they were said to have sighed in despair at their last view of Venice.

OLD LONDON BRIDGE, U.K.

There have been bridges over the river Thames in London for 2,000 years. One of the most famous is the Old London Bridge. It took 33 years to build and was so expensive that when it was finished in 1209, King John had to sell off plots for people to build on. Some of the buildings were seven stories tall, and overhung the road that crossed the bridge.

BROOKLYN BRIDGE, U.S.

On May 24, 1883, Brooklyn Bridge in New York City was opened. Soon after there were worries that it might collapse, so a parade of 21 elephants was led across the bridge to prove it was safe! At 5,988 ft (1,825 m) long, it was the world's first-ever steel-wire suspension bridge. It remained the longest of its kind for 20 years.

GOLDEN GATE BRIDGE, U.S.

The Golden Gate channel, which connects San Francisco Bay in California to the Pacific Ocean, was once thought far too dangerous to bridge. Yet, after four years of working in often treacherous conditions, this beautiful six-lane, steel suspension bridge was opened in 1937.

▼ Pont du Gard in France is the highest of all Roman aqueducts, with three tall tiers of arches.

PONT DU GARD CONTAINS 50,400 TONS (45,722 TONNES) OF LIMESTONE WITH SOME BLOCKS WEIGHING UP TO 6 TONS (5.44 TONNES) EACH.

SYDNEY HARBOUR BRIDGE, AUSTRALIA

Sydney didn't have a bridge across its harbor until 1924, when a contract was awarded to a British firm. The design was a simple steel arch that could carry six lanes of road traffic, four railroad and tram tracks, and two walkways. It opened on March 19, 1932 and is still the tallest steel arch in existence at 160 ft (49 m) wide, 440 ft (134 m) tall, and 3,770 ft (1,149 m) long.

PONT DU GARD, FRANCE

◄ ROMAN INGENUITY

Around AD 40, Roman engineers constructed a 165-mi- (265-km-) long aqueduct, or channel, to carry water from a spring at Uzès to the city of Nîmes. Unfortunately the Gardon River blocked its path. The Romans solved this problem by constructing a 1,180-ft- (360-m-) long aqueduct that was supported on three tiers of arches 160 ft (49 m) tall. When it was complete, the bridge carried nearly 7,000 cu ft (200,000 cu m) of water every day to fill the fountains, baths, and basins of Nîmes.

MEGA Rome

There was never a dull moment in the city of Rome. The emperor put on plenty of entertainment for his subjects to keep them occupied. There were two vast stadia—the Colosseum, where gladiators fought and wild animals were killed, and an oval track known as the Circus Maximus, where chariots raced.

CIRCUS MAXIMUS PRESENTS

A DAY AT THE RACES

- THIS SUNDAY AT NOON
- FREE ENTRANCE!

WHAT A VENUE!

To this day, the Circus Maximus remains the largest sports stadium ever built—it was able to accommodate 250,000 spectators. Four teams of chariots—the Reds, Whites, Greens, and Blues, all owned by the emperor—raced seven times around the track, a total of about 5 mi (8 km). The sharp corners at the end of each straight were incredibly dangerous—crashes were common and injuries often serious.

Chariot drivers wore helmets but no other protective clothing as they raced at great speeds around the track.

A THRILLING RIDE!

Usually a team of horses pulled each lightweight chariot, but camels and elephants sometimes took their place. The charioteer wrapped the reins around himself to avoid falling out. He also carried a sharp dagger to cut himself free if the chariot turned upside down and trapped him.

The oval track was an impressive 1,780 ft (542 m) long and 460 ft (140 m) wide.

Tiered seating was split up into zones by walkways

Shrines and monuments sat along the central *spina*—the area that divided the track

RACE DAY! CAN YOU PICK A WINNER?

COME ON REDS!

THE COLOSSEUM!

In AD 80, thousands of Romans turned up to the Colosseum for a gladiator festival lasting 100 days. This new four-tiered oval stadium was 617 ft (188 m) long, 512 ft (156 m) wide, and 131 ft (40 m) high. A typical day's events began with a parade of gladiators, dancers, and musicians. It continued with fights between armed hunters and wild animals, and then ended with the most popular events— gladiator contests.

The Colosseum could seat up to 50,000 people.

MAIN EVENT: GLADIATORS PRISCUS AND VERUS GO HEAD TO HEAD!

A defeated gladiator on the ground appeals for mercy from the crowd—the victor looks up as he awaits instruction to kill or spare his rival.

ENTER THE ARENA

Gladiators were usually prisoners of war, criminals, or slaves, with the occasional volunteer. They trained hard and fought each other with swords and tridents. If a gladiator was wounded, he could appeal to either the referee or the emperor to stop the fight. The audience made their views known with cheers or boos. Often the gladiator was spared, as gladiators were expensive to train.

FREE ENTRY!

GRAND OPENING AD LXXX!

VERUS FOR VICTOR!

GET HIM PRISCUS!

Holy WISDOM

For nearly 1,000 years after its construction in AD 537, Hagia Sophia was one of the largest churches in the world. Yet this beautiful holy place was nearly destroyed by two earthquakes, and was ransacked by Christian Crusaders in 1204. It was then attacked by Muslim armies in 1453, but it survived, and continues to dominate the skyline of Istanbul, Turkey, today.

AFTER TURKEY BECAME A REPUBLIC IN 1923, ISTANBUL BECAME THE OFFICIAL NAME FOR CONSTANTINOPLE.

▷ Measuring 269 ft (82 m) long and 240 ft (73 m) wide, the church stands 180 ft (55 m) tall.

A mighty city

In AD 330, Emperor Constantine ordered the capital of the Roman Empire to be moved east from Rome to the ancient Greek city of Byzantium. The city was renamed Constantinople in his honor and soon became the largest and wealthiest city in Europe. First, it was the capital of the Roman Empire and then of the Byzantine Empire. In 1453 the city fell to the Ottoman Turks and became the capital of their vast empire.

◁ Justinian the Great ruled the Byzantine Empire from AD 527 until AD 565. He ordered many fine buildings, including Hagia Sophia, to be erected in Constantinople.

Domes and minarets

The name Hagia Sophia means "Holy Wisdom." The building is dominated by its massive dome, which rests on top of 40 arched windows. The windows let sunlight into the building, giving the dome the appearance of hovering in light. After the church became a mosque in 1453, minarets (towers) were built at each of its four corners.

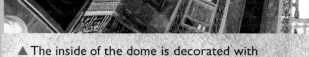
▲ The inside of the dome is decorated with inscriptions from the Qu'ran, the holy book of Islam.

▲ The beautiful interior of Hagia Sophia when it was in use as a place of worship.

Third time lucky

The church we see today is actually the third to be built at the site. It was completed by AD 537 after the two previous buildings had burnt down. This new church was larger and far more splendid than its predecessors. No expense was spared in its construction—green marble was shipped from Thessaly in Greece, purple porphyry from Egypt, yellow stone from Syria, black stone from Turkey, and Greek columns from the Temple of Artemis at Ephesus.

CHANGES OVER TIME

AD 537 Hagia Sophia is originally built as a Greek Orthodox basilica (church). In AD 558, the main dome collapses during an earthquake and is rebuilt. In AD 859 a great fire causes much damage, as do earthquakes in AD 869 and AD 989.

1204 Christian Crusaders on their way to liberate the Holy Land from Muslim rule ransack Constantinople and turn the church into a Roman Catholic cathedral.

1261 Byzantines recapture Constantinople and return Hagia Sophia to Greek Orthodox control.

1453 After the Muslim Ottomans seize Constantinople, Hagia Sophia becomes a mosque—four minarets are built at each corner. The mosque is restored in 1739-1740 and then once again in 1847-1849.

1935 Mustafa Kemal Atatürk, the president of Turkey, turns Hagia Sophia into a museum.

City in THE CLOUDS

The Incas of South America were master masons. They cut and shaped their building stones so perfectly that even a blade of grass could not fit between them. The Incas manually dragged these huge stones into place with rollers. The Inca Empire was conquered in 1532 by the Spanish conquistadors and little of its grandeur survives today. The mystical city of Machu Picchu, however, remained intact.

Sacred site

The city of Machu Picchu stands 7,970 ft (2,430 m) above sea level on a saddle of flat land between two mountains above the Sacred Valley, about 50 mi (80 km) from Cusco, Peru. The city has 200 buildings arranged on wide terraces around a vast central square. These buildings include palaces, temples, and simple houses. Machu Picchu stands in an earthquake zone, so the Incas built its walls without mortar, allowing the carefully fitted stones to move and then settle again should an earthquake strike.

Building an empire

In around 1200 the Incas of Peru began to build a vast empire. By the 1470s it stretched 1,985 mi (3,195 km) down the western side of South America, from what is now Ecuador in the north, to Chile in the south. The Incas were great builders, constructing huge fortresses and a vast network of roads measuring at least 12,500 mi (20,117 km) long. They terraced their steep hillside for farming, and built many bridges over the steep valleys.

▼ The road to Machu Picchu zigzags up the steep mountainside.

FANTASTIC FEATURES

Machu Picchu is home to many stone temples, as well as the Intihuatana stone, which works like a calendar. At midday on November 11 and January 30, the Sun is directly overhead and casts no shadow. On June 21—when the Sun is at its highest—the stone casts a shadow on its southern side, while on December 21—when it is at its lowest—a shorter shadow falls on its northern side.

▶ Machu Picchu was founded around 1450, but abandoned in the 1570s after the Spanish had conquered the Inca Empire. This artwork shows Hiram Bingham viewing the city, covered in vegetation, for the first time.

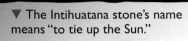

▼ The Intihuatana stone's name means "to tie up the Sun."

Rediscovered at last

The Spanish conquistadors never discovered Machu Picchu. But in 1572 they introduced smallpox to Peru, possibly causing an epidemic that wiped out Machu Picchu's inhabitants. The ruined city then remained undisturbed until July 24, 1911, when the American archeologist Hiram Bingham rediscovered it.

▶ At the Temple of the Condor is a rock that has been carved into the shape of a condor—an enormous flying bird.

▲ The Temple of the Three Windows was dedicated to the Sun god Inti, the greatest Inca god.

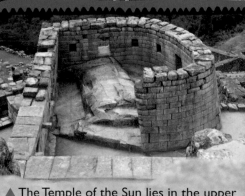

▲ The Temple of the Sun lies in the upper part of the town, which was used mainly for religious and ceremonial purposes.

Sacred TEMPLE

Deep in the jungles of Cambodia in Southeast Asia lies one of the most remarkable temples in the world. Angkor Wat was built during the reign of King Suryavarman II, who ruled Cambodia from 1113 to 1150. The temple was built to honor the Hindu god Vishnu, but during the late 1200s the country—and the temple—became Buddhist.

▼ Angkor Wat rises from the jungle, which for centuries has threatened to completely engulf it.

Building the temple

Stone for the temple was quarried at Mount Kulen, about 25 mi (40 km) from the site. It was then carried by raft along the Siem Reap River. More than 5.6 million tons (5 million tonnes) of sandstone was used—as much stone as the Great Pyramid at Giza.

▼ Angkor Wat is surrounded by a moat of water kept at a constant height. If the water were to rise or fall, the stone walls of the temple would crack and collapse.

Mountain peaks

As well as being a masterpiece of construction, Angkor Wat's architecture is thought to be symbolic. The temple itself may represent Mount Meru, home of the gods. The five towers are thought to symbolize the mountain's five peaks, with the walls and moats representing its surrounding mountains and oceans. Inside, the three main galleries represent Brahma—the god of creation, the moon, and Vishnu—the Supreme Being. Another theory is that Angkor Wat was designed to represent peace, while others believe it represents the star constellation Draco (dragon).

▶ Vishnu is the supreme god of Hinduism and is usually shown with four arms, just visible on this damaged statue.

A complex design

Angkor Wat is surrounded by a 625-ft- (190-m-) wide moat and a high outer wall. This wall encloses a large area, which originally contained not only the temple but also a royal palace and town. A 1,150-ft- (350-m-) long causeway leads to the temple itself, which stands on a raised terrace. The temple consists of three rectangular galleries—the outer one is 613 ft (187 m) by 705 ft (215 m).

The temple's outer wall is an enormous 3,360 ft (1,024 m) long and 2,632 ft (802 m) wide

The tower at the center of Angkor Wat is 213 ft (65 m) tall

A sandstone causeway links the temple to surrounding areas

▲ Angkor Wat was built in just 40 years. The stone was hauled into place by elephants using bamboo scaffolding, ropes, and pulleys.

▶ Enormous carvings and stone figures of devata (or gods) and apsaras (female spirits of the clouds and waters), decorate the temple.

Covered in carvings

Angkor Wat's walls are carved with scenes from the epic Hindu poems the *Ramayana* and the *Mahabharata*. Many of the ceilings are carved with snakes, lions, and garudas (birdlike creatures). Statues of Vishnu and other Hindu gods are also placed around the temple.

Worship and WONDER

In many cities the most impressive building is a Christian cathedral. With their high towers and spires, these beautiful structures reach to the heavens and dominate the city below. Often filled with magnificent treasures, cathedrals are places of worship and wonder, a stone and glass recognition of the many talented workmen who constructed them.

Westminster Abbey

One of the most important churches in the U.K. is Westminster Abbey, which stands in the middle of London. Every king since Harold II in 1066 has been crowned in the Abbey, and many of them have been married here too. Many famous Britons are buried here, including The Unknown Warrior, an unidentified British solider killed during World War I (1914–1918).

▼ The two towers at the western end of Westminster Abbey were designed by famous architect Nicholas Hawksmoor and erected between 1722 and 1745.

◀ King George IV was crowned in much splendor at Westminster Abbey in 1821. His disgraced wife Queen Caroline was excluded from the ceremony.

Chartres Cathedral

Many people consider Chartres Cathedral in France to be the most impressive in the world. It was mostly built between 1194 and 1250. The nave, or main body, of the church is 121 ft (37 m) tall, while the two western towers are 344 ft (105 m) and 371 ft (113 m) high. They are visible for miles across the countryside. Set high up in the walls are 176 richly colored stained-glass windows depicting religious scenes.

▼ On the floor of the cathedral is an elaborate labyrinth, or maze, picked out in colored stone. It represents Jerusalem, the Christian holy city.

◀ At night, the walls of the cathedral are lit up, illuminating the impressive architecture.

◀ Many beautiful—and enormous—stained-glass windows adorn Chartres Cathedral. The north Rose window, shown here, is 34 ft (10.4 m) across.

The dome of St. Peter's in Rome is the tallest dome in the world.

St. Peter's Basilica

The main center of the Roman Catholic Church is St. Peter's Basilica in Rome. This vast church was built between 1506 and 1626, and features an enormous dome standing 453 ft (138 m) above the ground. The church and its buildings are so large, they form an independent nation—Vatican City—the smallest independent state in the world.

▲ On Sundays and other religious occasions, the Pope addresses Catholics from his balcony, which overlooks the square.

CRUSADER Castle

For hundreds of years, warriors built massive stone castles to protect themselves from their enemies. Krak des Chevaliers in Syria was one such castle, strategically fortified to defend against siege during the Crusades—a series of military campaigns undertaken to regain control over Jerusalem and the Holy Land.

Designed for defense

Krak des Chevaliers commanded the main route from Syria into the Holy Land. The original Muslim fortress fell to the Crusaders in 1099, and in 1144 it was taken over by the Knights Hospitallers, who rebuilt it in the form we see today. The knights strengthened the castle, surrounding the fortified inner settlement with a lower, outer wall over which they could shoot at an attacking enemy.

▶ Today, Krak des Chevaliers is remarkably well-preserved, and still stands almost intact on its rocky hilltop.

The Crusades

In 1095 Pope Urban II issued a call to arms. The Muslim Turks who controlled Jerusalem were now preventing European pilgrims from visiting the holy sites. He asked for an army to reclaim the land for Christians. Thousands of Crusaders answered his call, seizing Jerusalem in 1099 and ruling the area until the Muslims retook it by 1291.

▼ This illustrated manuscript shows a French army loading supplies onto a ship as they prepare to depart for the Holy Land.

FRENCH FORTRESS

Richard I of England once owned many estates in northern France, and in 1195–1198 he built Château Gaillard to defend them. The castle stood on a spur of rock above the River Seine. Richard boasted that he could hold the castle, "even if the walls were made of butter." Yet in 1204, Philip II of France surrounded the castle. His troops undermined one of the outer walls and rushed in, taking everyone inside prisoner.

▼ Château Gaillard was once an imposing fortress, dominating the region. Today, its ruins are still substantial.

Inside the walls

If an enemy managed to breach Krak des Chevalier's outer walls, the defending knights could retreat inside the inner walls and continue to fight. Numerous towers gave the knights lookout points to see the enemy. The entrance to the castle was through a narrow, covered passage that snaked up the side of the hill. An enemy would have to force a way through the passage in order to get inside the castle.

Entrance

Armory

Barbican, or Approach Tower

Chapel

Farmyard

Stores

Great Hall

Kitchens

Stables

Refectory

Aqueduct

The crucial weakness

The castle could only be approached from one direction, making it almost impossible to invade—yet Krak des Chevaliers had one fatal flaw. All water flowed into the castle along a single aqueduct from the surrounding hills. Cut the aqueduct and the castle would quickly run out of water. A Muslim siege failed to break into the castle in 1188, but in 1270 a vast Egyptian army cut off its water. The 200 knights inside held out for six weeks, but the enemy managed to damage the outer walls and break in. The knights surrendered, and the inhabitants left the castle alive.

▶ The badge of the Knights Hospitaller was a white Maltese cross on a black background.

WHO WERE THE HOSPITALLERS?

The Order of Hospitallers was established in around 1023 to care for sick, injured, and poor pilgrims who had come from Europe to visit the Holy Land. After the Crusader conquest of Jerusalem in 1099, the knights took over the defense of the Holy Land until Muslim forces expelled them in 1291.

HEROIC Statues

233 ft (71 m)

People who live near the statue say, "the mountain is a Buddha and Buddha is a mountain."

26 ft (8 m)

Most of the moai weigh about 14 tons (12.7 tonnes) each, but the heaviest statue is a massive 86 tons (78 tonnes)!

Leshan Buddha

Moai statues

Around the globe, many massive statues dominate our landscapes. These colossal carvings are awe-inspiring for their immensity. They each have a story to tell, even though they cannot speak—they can remind people of their faith, or an important event in their past.

Where the Min, Dadu, and Qingyi rivers meet near Leshan in Sichuan province, China, the water is highly dangerous for boats. In AD 713, a Chinese monk called Haitong decided to carve a large Buddha in the nearby cliff to calm the waters. He was so determined to complete his task that when he ran out of money, he gouged out his eyes to show his seriousness. After his death, his followers completed the project in AD 803. The statue of a seated Buddha is vast—its shoulders are 92 ft (28 m) wide.

Only 5,761 people live on Rapa Nui (Easter Island) in the eastern Pacific Ocean. They share their home with 887 moai—stone statues with human features. The carvings were made between 1100 and 1600, and stand in rows on stone platforms known as *ahu* around the coastline. The population of Rapa Nui collapsed in the 18th century, perhaps due in part to deforestation—the islanders cut down their trees to help move the statues into position.

98 ft (30 m)

This statue cost the equivalent of $3,300,000 (just under £2,000,000) when it was built in the 1930s.

279 ft (85 m)

When this massive statue was dedicated in 1967, it was the tallest sculpture in the world.

THE STATUE OF LIBERTY CARRIES LAWS IN HER LEFT HAND AND THE TORCH OF FREEDOM IN HER RIGHT HAND.

305 ft (93 m)

The seven rays that surround the statue's head represent the Sun, the seven seas, and the seven continents.

Christ the Redeemer

In 1931 the devout Roman Catholics of Rio de Janeiro, Brazil, put up the fifth largest statue of Christ in the world. It was placed on top of the 2,297-ft- (700-m-) high Corcovado mountain, which overlooks the city. The statue itself stands on top of a 26 ft (8 m) pedestal and its outstretched arms span an enormous 92 ft (28 m). The whole statue, which is made of reinforced concrete and soapstone, weighs 711 tons (645 tonnes).

The Motherland Calls

More than 1,150,000 Russians were killed or injured during the brutal Battle of Stalingrad in 1942–1943, during World War II (1939–1945). In 1967 a statue known as The Motherland Calls was erected in Volgograd, Russia, to honor their memory. The statue, which shows a woman with a sword in her hand, represents the motherland of Russia. It weighs 8,700 tons (7,893 tonnes). Two hundred steps, representing two hundred days of battle, lead to the statue.

Statue of Liberty

As you approach New York, U.S., by sea, as generations of immigrants from Europe have done, the vast Statue of Liberty looms up over you. This famous iron and copper statue was made in France and then shipped in crates across the Atlantic to be assembled, and then raised up on its stone pedestal. Designed by Frédéric Auguste Bartholdi, it was given to the U.S. by the people of France in 1886 to celebrate American independence.

MAYAN Masterpiece

When the Spanish conquistadors took over the Yucatán Peninsula of Mexico in 1532, they were amazed to discover a city as grand as anything in Europe. The city of Chichén Itzá was built between AD 750 and AD 998 by the Maya, the remarkably educated and intelligent people who lived in the area. The city was vast, filled with temples and other fine buildings.

▶ The Great Ball Court was by the far the largest of the 13 ball courts in Chichén Itzá.

A developed city

The city of Chichén Itzá covers a large area—at least 2 sq mi (5 sq km). Creating space for the city was no mean feat—the ground had to be leveled for the many temples, ball courts, warehouses, stores, houses, and other buildings. A network of paved causeways linked the structures together. The name of the city means "at the mouth of the well of the Itzá" in the Maya language.

▼ The Maya built large cities, such as Chichén Itzá, with stepped pyramid temples. They traded gold, jade, and other precious stones with their neighbors.

A Great Ball Court
B Temple of Kukulkan (El Castillo)
C Observatory
D Skull Platform
E The Plaza of a Thousand Columns
F Temple of the Warriors
G Temple of the Jaguars
H Ossuary (burial site)

A The Great Ball Court

The Maya played a game using a solid, rubber ball. The exact rules are not known, but it is likely that the aim was to keep the ball up in the air for play to continue. Measuring 551 ft (168 m) by 230 ft (70 m), the court is far longer than a modern soccer pitch. It is surrounded on two sides by high walls, on which there are rings carved with feathered serpents. Perhaps the aim was to throw the ball through one of these rings. It is likely that prisoners were forced to play the ball game and then beheaded when they lost.

C Observing the stars

The Maya settled in the Yucatán Peninsula of Mexico around 800 BC and soon created a thriving society. They were fine mathematicians, devising the concept of zero and observing the heavens to predict solar eclipses and other events.

▶ The observatory at Chichén Itzá is known as *El Caracol*, which means "the snail."

▲ Rows of skulls were carved along the wall of a large platform.

B The mighty temple

Dominating Chichén Itzá is the Temple of Kukulkan, often referred to as *El Castillo*, which means "the castle." Kukulkan was a feathered serpent god. His temple is vast, standing 98 ft (30 m) high and consisting of nine square terraces rising up to the top. In the 1930s archeologists discovered that there was another, older temple buried underneath it. Inside was a chamber with a throne in the shape of a jaguar, painted red with spots of inlaid jade.

▼ In the late afternoon of the spring and fall equinoxes, the Sun casts a series of triangular shadows down the northwest side of the Kukulkan, which looks like a serpent wriggling down a staircase.

D The skull platform

Structures around the city show how brutal the Maya could be. The *Tzompantli*, or Skull Platform, displays the skulls of their victims while the nearby Platform of the Eagles and the Jaguars has carved panels showing those animals eating human hearts. To the north of the city lies the Sacred Cenote, a natural well in which people were sacrificed to the gods.

RUSSIAN Fortress

At the heart of the Russian capital of Moscow lies a vast fortress, home to the all-powerful president and before him the tsars of Russia. From within its secretive walls, these powerful rulers have plotted against their enemies and sent armies around the world. This is the seat of all Russian power.

КРАСНАЯ
ПЛОЩАДЬ

The Tsar Bell

At the exact center of Moscow stands the impressive Ivan the Great Bell Tower. It looks like a 268-ft- (81-m-) tall burning candle. The tower used to be the tallest building in Moscow, as construction of higher buildings was once prohibited. The tower has 21 bells, which were rung if the city was in danger. Sitting next to the tower is the Tsar Bell, the largest bell in the world. It is made of bronze, weighs 445,166 lb (201,924 kg), and is 20.1 ft (6.1 m) tall. Unfortunately, it has never been rung—it was broken during casting.

◀ The Tsar Bell sits next to the impressive bell tower that would have housed it, had it not broken.

The First Kremlin

The Kremlin sits on Borovitsky Hill, where the Neglinnaya River flows into the Moskva River. The site was first fortified in the AD 900s. Prince Yuri Dolgoruky expanded the fortifications in 1156, only to see the whole fortress burned down by the Mongols in 1237. In 1339 a new, oak-walled fortress was erected, with a church, monastery, and cathedral inside the walls. In 1366–1368 Dmitri Donskoi, son of Ivan II, replaced the oak walls with white limestone. During the reign of Ivan III (1462–1505), a new palace was built for the Russian tsars. The Kremlin has been the center of Russian government ever since.

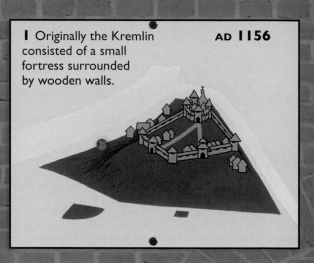

1 Originally the Kremlin consisted of a small fortress surrounded by wooden walls. **AD 1156**

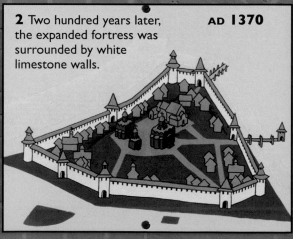

2 Two hundred years later, the expanded fortress was surrounded by white limestone walls. **AD 1370**

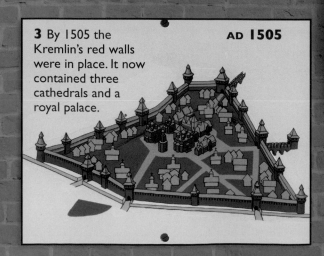

3 By 1505 the Kremlin's red walls were in place. It now contained three cathedrals and a royal palace. **AD 1505**

What's inside the walls?

The imposing Kremlin walls we see today were largely built between 1485 and 1495. They measure 7,332 ft (2,235 m) long, are between 11 ft (3.4 m) and 21 ft (6.4 m) thick, and up to 62 ft (19 m) tall. Along their length are 20 towers. The walls enclose a vast area of 68 acres (275,186 sq m). There are four cathedrals, two churches, five palaces, an armory for weapons, and numerous other buildings.

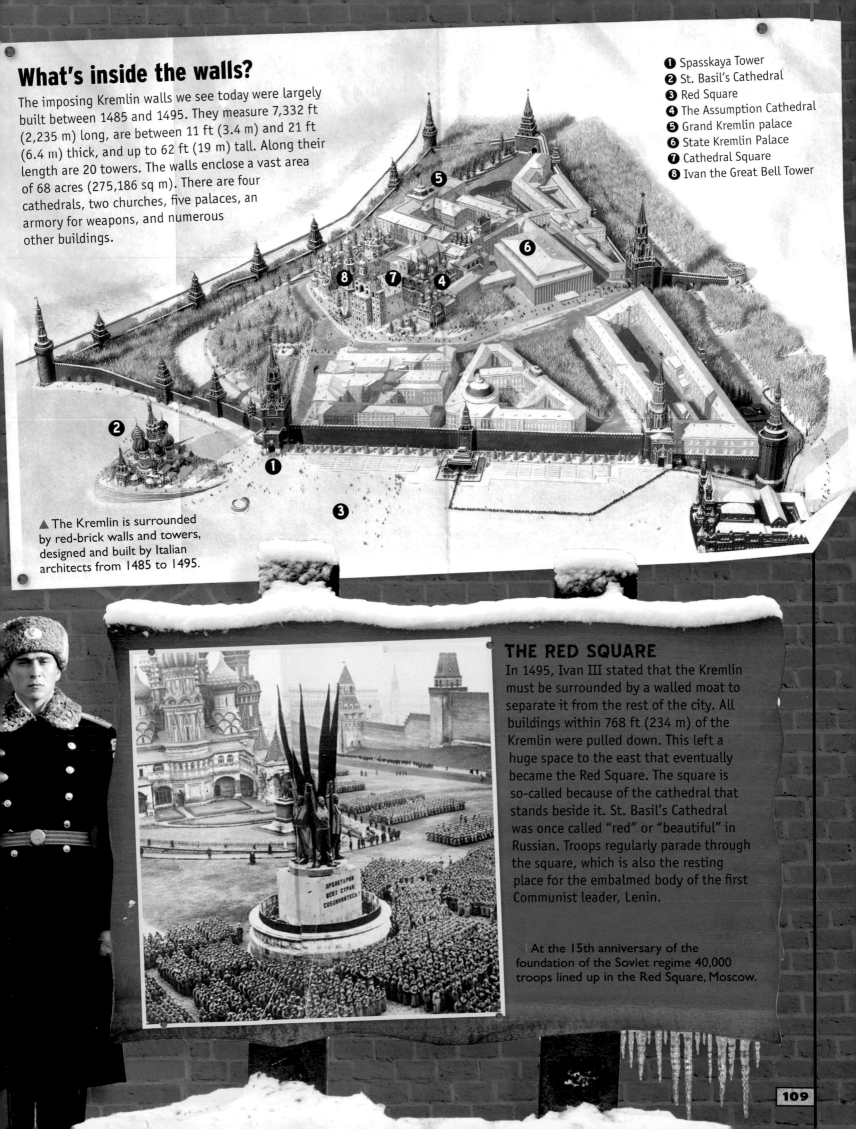

❶ Spasskaya Tower
❷ St. Basil's Cathedral
❸ Red Square
❹ The Assumption Cathedral
❺ Grand Kremlin palace
❻ State Kremlin Palace
❼ Cathedral Square
❽ Ivan the Great Bell Tower

▲ The Kremlin is surrounded by red-brick walls and towers, designed and built by Italian architects from 1485 to 1495.

THE RED SQUARE

In 1495, Ivan III stated that the Kremlin must be surrounded by a walled moat to separate it from the rest of the city. All buildings within 768 ft (234 m) of the Kremlin were pulled down. This left a huge space to the east that eventually became the Red Square. The square is so-called because of the cathedral that stands beside it. St. Basil's Cathedral was once called "red" or "beautiful" in Russian. Troops regularly parade through the square, which is also the resting place for the embalmed body of the first Communist leader, Lenin.

◀ At the 15th anniversary of the foundation of the Soviet regime 40,000 troops lined up in the Red Square, Moscow.

MUGHAL Majesty

One of the most spectacular buildings in the world, the perfectly symmetrical Taj Mahal is a monument to love, as well as a great feat of construction. Due to varying levels of light throughout the day, the white marble exterior can appear to change color. In the morning it seems to be a shade of pink, and it looks golden in the moonlight.

The jewel of India

The Taj Mahal sits on a large marble base by the river Yamuna near the city of Agra, which was the capital of Mughal India. The building itself is roughly 180 sq ft (17 sq m), and on each of its four sides are vaulted archways. One of its most recognizable features is the onion-shaped dome on top, which reaches 250 ft (76 m) in height. Four minarets measuring 130 ft (40 m) tall, stand at each corner, and beautiful water gardens surround the building.

▶ The Taj Mahal is set in a 980-sq-ft (91-sq-m) formal garden that contains avenues of trees, fountains, and pools of water.

Decorated spire

Drum-shaped support for the dome

One of four *chattris* (small domes) placed at each corner of the main dome

Guldasta (decorative spire)

Minaret, a tall thin tower used by *muezzins* (callers) to summon worshipers to prayer

Decorated spandrel (space around the arch)

Precious stones

The marble used to build the Taj Mahal was brought to the site by 1,000 elephants from more than 300 mi (483 km) away. Twenty thousand Indian workers labored for 20 years to complete the building. They all had different skills—some carved the marble flowers, while others built the turrets. The workers decorated the walls in flower patterns made from 28 different types of semiprecious and precious stones, such as crystal and lapis lazuli. Some of the stones came from as far away as Arabia and Tibet.

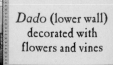

Dado (lower wall) decorated with flowers and vines

◀ The scale of the Taj Mahal is made even more impressive by its intricate details, such as these jeweled flowers.

Emperor Shah Jahan

Shah Jahan ruled the Mughal Empire of India from 1628 until 1658, extending Mughal power to the south and capturing the important city of Kandahar from the Persians. He supported the arts, erecting many fine buildings during his reign. In 1612 Shah Jahan married Arjumand Banu Begum, the daughter of a Persian noble family, who served the emperors. They had 14 children together, seven of whom survived into adulthood. In 1631 she died during childbirth, and the emperor was overwhelmed with grief—he built the Taj Mahal as a tomb for her.

Onion-shaped dome

◀ Shah Jahan loved his wife very much. She became known as Mumtaz Mahal, which means "the chosen one of the palace."

Pishtaq (vaulted archway)

▼ The memorial to Mumtaz Mahal is found to the right of her husband's cenotaph.

Calligraphy (decorative writing)

Two tombs together

The two cenotaphs, or memorials, to Mumtaz Mahal and Shah Jahan lie in a chamber directly underneath the main dome of the Taj Mahal. Both the memorials and the chamber itself are heavily decorated in marble and semiprecious stones. The bodies of Mumtaz and Jahan are buried in caskets in a second crypt, or chamber, underneath. Muslims forbid graves to be elaborately decorated, so the crypt is lined with simple sheets of marble. The caskets are inlaid with precious stones and calligraphy praising Mumtaz.

Palace of Versailles

King Louis XIV of France called himself "the Sun King." He believed that the Kingdom of France revolved around him in the same way that Earth revolves around the Sun. Louis wanted to show off this immense power and majesty, so he had a magnificent palace built. At Versailles, Louis lived in extraordinary splendor. The building itself was enormous, and was filled with lavishly decorated rooms.

▼ The Palace of Versailles is surrounded by almost 2,000 acres (809 hectares) of gardens.

▲ Louis reigned France from 1643 until 1715. He became king at just four years old.

How big?

It is difficult to imagine the sheer scale of Versailles. The total floor area of the palace is 721,182 sq ft (67,000 sq m), the equivalent of almost ten full-sized soccer pitches. It has 2,300 rooms, 67 staircases, and 2,153 windows, and contains 5,210 items of furniture, more than 6,000 paintings, and 2,000 sculptures. The palace is so large that members of the French aristocracy who lived there were moved from room to room in sedan chairs, carried by footmen.

The growing palace

The Palace of Versailles outside Paris was once a small hunting lodge. The young French king, Louis XIV, fell in love with the countryside there and began to expand the lodge into his own palace. Work begun in 1664 and carried on in four main stages until 1710. Later monarchs added more rooms and built further palaces in the grounds.

The hall of mirrors

At the heart of the palace is a vast chamber known as the Hall of Mirrors (below). This great hall is 239.5 ft (73 m) long, 34.4 ft (10.5 m) wide, and 40.4 ft (12.3 m) high. It is lined with 357 mirrors and lit with beautiful lamps and hanging chandeliers. Louis XIV walked along the hall every day from his private apartments to the chapel and back again. Courtiers lined the route to watch him pass.

Marie Antoinette

One of the most famous residents of Versailles was Queen Marie Antoinette, wife of Louis XVI. In 1784 she built herself a mock village in the grounds, with 12 cottages and a mill. Here she escaped the formality of life at Versailles. She dressed up as a peasant and milked the cows, which had previously been scrubbed clean by her staff. The real peasants of France were not amused, and in 1789 they started a revolution that overthrew the king and queen. Marie Antoinette was executed by guillotine in 1793.

▼ In the ground of Versailles, Marie Antoinette constructed a peasant village to entertain herself.

Brutal BATTLES

Discover the facts behind battles that have become legend. From supreme bravery to extreme brutality—this is the no-holds-barred account.

◀ Plate armor was not easily penetrated by even the strongest swords, so combatants aimed for any weak points, or delivered blows with crushing weapons, such as maces.

CHARIOT Warfare

In May 1274 BC, two massive armies came together by the river Orontes near Kadesh, Syria. Egyptian Pharaoh Ramesses II led an army of 2,000 war chariots and 20,000 men. The larger Hittite army had 3,500 chariots and 50,000 men. Thousands were killed in the largest chariot battle ever fought.

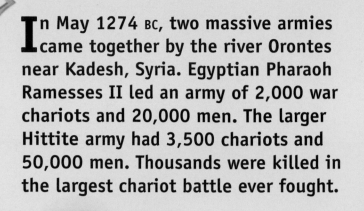

RAMESSES II

One of the most important pharaohs of ancient Egypt, Ramesses II (1303–1213 BC) became king in 1279 BC, aged 25, and ruled for 66 years. He waged war against the Hittites to the north and the Libyans to the west. In paintings and carvings, he was often shown leading his troops into battle on his war chariot. Among the many temples he built were two vast constructions carved out of the solid rock at Abu Simbel by the river Nile.

Battle by the river

Ramesses II and the lead division of the Egyptian army advanced north toward Kadesh. They thought the Hittites were further north and set up camp. The Hittites, however, were hidden on the other side of the river Orontes—where they launched a surprise ambush on the rest of the Egyptian army, before attacking the camp. As more Hittite chariots crossed the river, Ramesses II mounted a counterattack. The battle swung to and fro until both sides withdrew. Many of the Hittites drowned in the river Orontes as they fled.

▲ At the Battle of Kadesh, Ramesses II drove his chariot into battle. Normally he would have had a driver in the chariot with him.

EGYPTIANS VS. HITTITES

1700s BC	Hittites establish large empire in what is now central Turkey
1295 BC	Muwatalli II becomes king of the Hittites
1279 BC	Ramesses II rules Egypt
1274 BC	**Ramesses II leads Egyptians against the Hittites at the Battle of Kadesh**
1272 BC	Death of Muwatalli II
1264 BC	Construction of vast twin temples at Abu Simbel in southern Egypt begins
1258 BC	Ramesses II signs a peace treaty with King Hattusili III, the new Hittite king
1213 BC	Death of Ramesses II, who was buried in the Valley of the Kings

◀ The peace treaty has been preserved on stone tablets.

Time for peace

After the battle was over, Ramesses II declared he had won a great victory. However, neither side had won. The Hittites occupied two northern Egyptian provinces in Lebanon while Ramesses returned to Egypt. In 1258, Ramesses signed a peace treaty with the Hittite king Hattusili III to end the war. This was the first time in history that such a treaty had been signed between two former enemies.

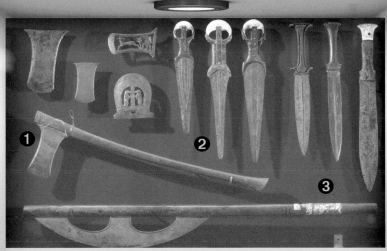

EGYPTIAN WEAPONS
❶ Battle ax ❷ Daggers with ivory handles ❸ Epsilon-shaped ax

Attack and defense

The main weapon of the Egyptians was a wooden bow, strengthened with horn. Its wooden arrows had tips of bronze, iron, or bone and could be fired to a distance of 575 ft (175 m). Soldiers on both sides also fought with axes, long and short swords, and bronze hatchets. They protected themselves with simple bronze shields.

WHEELED WAR VEHICLES

Drawn by two horses, the lightweight wooden chariot had two widely spaced, six-spoked wheels and a platform for the crew to stand on—one to steer and the other to fight. A well-driven chariot could reach a speed of up to 24 mph (38 km/h) and turn sharp corners with ease.

Battle of MARATHON

In 490 BC, King Darius I, leader of the powerful Persian Empire, decided to crush his rebellious Greek subjects. He assembled a massive force of about 25,000 men. They set sail across the Aegean Sea in a fleet of 600 triremes—large ships powered by three banks of oars. The battle that took place at Marathon ended Darius' dreams—the Greek troops overwhelmed the larger Persian army.

The attack

The Persian fleet landed at Marathon, close to their main target of Athens. Its force of 25,000 men outnumbered the Greeks two to one. Greek commander Miltiades arranged his hoplites into a long, thin phalanx that advanced at the enemy. The Greeks overwhelmed the Persian flanks, or ends. Greek troops in the center, however, came under Persian arrow fire and began to crumble. Seeing they were in trouble, more Greeks rushed in, causing the Persian force to collapse and retreat.

▼ The close formation of the Greek soldiers enabled them to swamp the Persians, leading to a decisive victory.

▼ In the phalanx formation, enemy soldiers could not get past the line of shields.

The ultimate formation

Greek soldiers were called hoplites. They went into battle armed with a long spear, a sword, and a large, round bronze shield. They wore bronze helmets, linen cuirasses (body armor), and greaves (shin guards). In battle, hoplites formed a tight-knit phalanx with their shields locked together around them and their spears raised.

GREEKS VS. PERSIANS

499 BC — Greeks in western Turkey revolt against Persian rule, but are soon crushed

490 BC — **Led by Darius I, Persians invade Greece but are defeated at the Battle of Marathon**

480 BC — Persians invade again, led by Xerxes, and defeat Greeks at the Battle of Thermopylae

480 BC — Greeks defeat Persian navy at Salamis

479 BC — Further Greek victories at Plataea and Mycale force Persians to withdraw invasion army from Greece

449 BC — Peace treaty is agreed to end the war

Escape by sea

By the end of the battle, the Persians had lost 6,400 men, the Greeks only 192. In a disorganized fashion, the remaining Persian army fled the battlefield, pursued by the Greeks. Some drowned in nearby swamps when trying to reach their large warships.

▶ About two thirds of the Persian army managed to board their ships and sail home to Asia.

The news runner

Greek legend states that after the Battle of Marathon, a messenger called Pheidippedes, who had just fought in the battle, ran home to Athens to announce the victory. He ran 26 mi (42 km) without stopping, bursting into the Athens assembly to announce, "We won." He then died. The modern-day marathon race commemorates Pheidippedes' achievement.

◀ A statue of Pheidippedes stands along the Olympic marathon route, near Athens.

ANCIENT GREEK SOLDIERS RARELY RODE HORSES BECAUSE IF THEY HURLED A SPEAR, THEY WERE LIKELY TO FALL OFF BACKWARD!

CONQUERING
the World

▲ Alexander leads his Macedonian cavalry over the river Granicus before attacking the Persians on the other bank.

Few people in history earn the title of "the Great," but one such man was Alexander. Aged 20, Alexander became king of Macedonia. He won three major victories to conquer the vast Persian Empire. He intended to invade India and the rest of the known world, but his troops wanted to return home to Macedonia. His dream of world domination did not come true.

GRANICUS, 334 BC

Alexander and his army of 43,000 infantry (foot soldiers) and 6,100 cavalry (horsemen) crossed the waterway that separated Greece from the Persian Empire in Asia. They crossed the river far from the main Persian army, only encountering a smaller Persian force by the river Granicus, outside Troy. The Persians had to quickly rearrange their troops, allowing Alexander's army to overwhelm them.

> ALEXANDER THE GREAT AND HIS ARMY MARCHED NEARLY 20,000 MI (32,000 KM) OVER THE COURSE OF HIS 11-YEAR CAMPAIGN.

ISSUS, 334 BC

After his victory at Granicus, Alexander moved south, freeing cities from Persian rule. A far larger Persian force, commanded by King Darius III, intercepted the Macedonian army at Issus, in what is now Turkey. Although the Macedonians were heavily outnumbered, they were stronger, well-trained soldiers. Darius abandoned the battle, leaving behind his mother, wife, two daughters, and large amounts of treasure.

▲ A Roman mosaic showing the Battle of Issus. Alexander (left) spears a Persian horseman as King Darius of Persia (far right) escapes on his chariot.

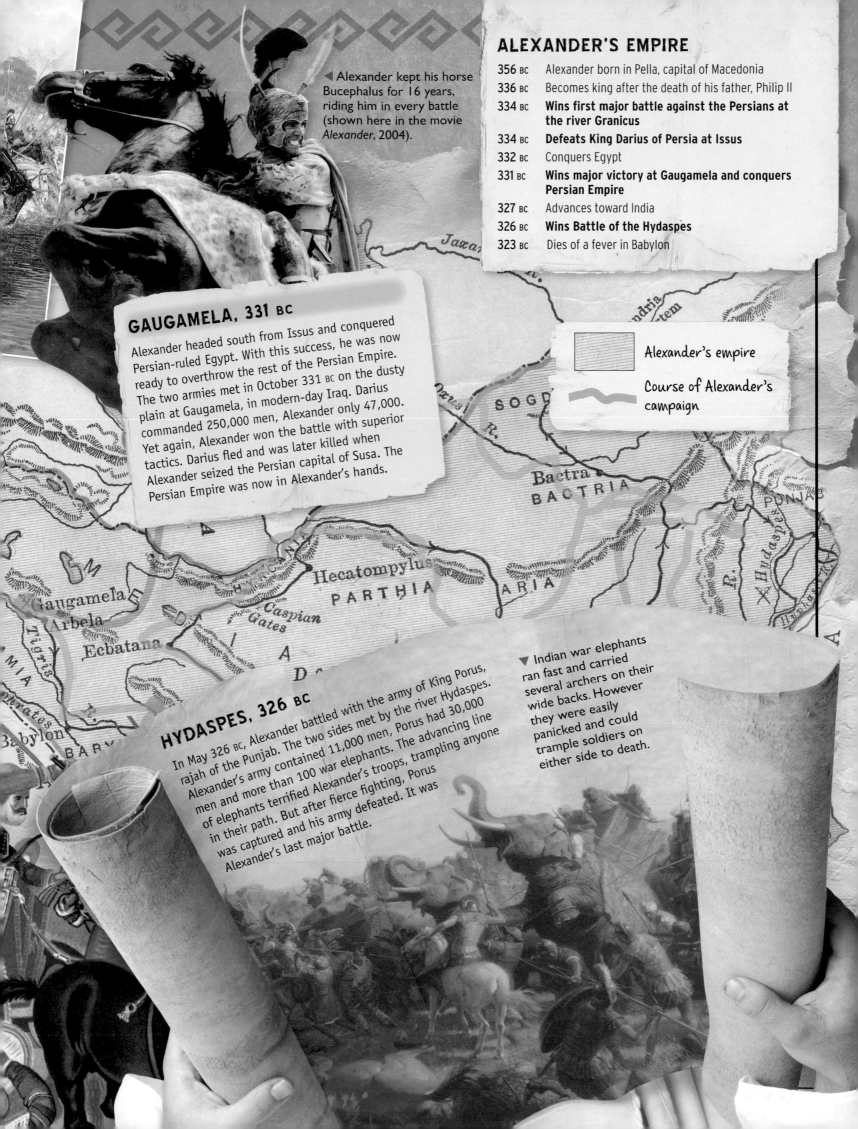

Alexander kept his horse Bucephalus for 16 years, riding him in every battle (shown here in the movie *Alexander*, 2004).

ALEXANDER'S EMPIRE

356 BC	Alexander born in Pella, capital of Macedonia
336 BC	Becomes king after the death of his father, Philip II
334 BC	**Wins first major battle against the Persians at the river Granicus**
334 BC	**Defeats King Darius of Persia at Issus**
332 BC	Conquers Egypt
331 BC	**Wins major victory at Gaugamela and conquers Persian Empire**
327 BC	Advances toward India
326 BC	**Wins Battle of the Hydaspes**
323 BC	Dies of a fever in Babylon

Alexander's empire

Course of Alexander's campaign

GAUGAMELA, 331 BC

Alexander headed south from Issus and conquered Persian-ruled Egypt. With this success, he was now ready to overthrow the rest of the Persian Empire. The two armies met in October 331 BC on the dusty plain at Gaugamela, in modern-day Iraq. Darius commanded 250,000 men, Alexander only 47,000. Yet again, Alexander won the battle with superior tactics. Darius fled and was later killed when Alexander seized the Persian capital of Susa. The Persian Empire was now in Alexander's hands.

HYDASPES, 326 BC

In May 326 BC, Alexander battled with the army of King Porus, rajah of the Punjab. The two sides met by the river Hydaspes. Alexander's army contained 11,000 men, Porus had 30,000 men and more than 100 war elephants. The advancing line of elephants terrified Alexander's troops, trampling anyone in their path. But after fierce fighting, Porus was captured and his army defeated. It was Alexander's last major battle.

▼ Indian war elephants ran fast and carried several archers on their wide backs. However they were easily panicked and could trample soldiers on either side to death.

DEADLIEST Days

For more than a century, the empires of Rome and Carthage fought three long and bloody wars—known as the Punic Wars—for control of the Mediterranean Sea. Of all the great battles fought, the Roman defeat at Cannae in 216 BC was one of the deadliest battles of all time.

ROMANS VS. CARTHAGINIANS

264–241 BC **First Punic War:** Rome and Carthage fight for control of Sicily. Carthage is defeated

260 BC Roman navy defeats Carthaginians at Mylae

218–201 BC **Second Punic War:** Carthage fights to avenge defeat in first war, but loses

218 BC Hannibal inflicts major defeat on the Romans at Trebia

217 BC Hannibal wins major battle at Lake Trasimene

216 BC Hannibal inflicts another massive defeat on the Romans at Cannae

149–146 BC **Third Punic War:** Rome inflicts final defeat of Carthage and razes city to the ground

▼ During the first Punic War, the Roman fleet defeated the Carthaginians at Mylae off the coast of Sicily.

First Punic War 264–241 BC

When Rome went to war with Carthage, Tunisia, in 264 BC to seize Sicily, Italy, its armies soon controlled the island but not the seas. Rome quickly built a fleet of triremes—boats with three tiers of oars—and developed the corvus—a long board with a spike underneath. When an enemy ship came close, the Romans dropped the corvus into its deck, allowing them to board the ship and kill the enemy. This innovation brought them success at Mylae in 260 BC. In 250 BC, the Romans invaded North Africa to end the war but were thrown out. Fighting dragged on until peace was made in 241 BC. Sicily became a Roman province.

▲ In 218 BC, the Carthaginian general Hannibal led 37 elephants and an army of 30,000 men across the Alps to launch a surprise attack on the Romans from the rear.

Second Punic War 218–201 BC

In July 216 BC, the Carthaginians seized a major Roman supply depot at Cannae in southern Italy. A Roman army of 86,000 soldiers set out to defeat them. The two armies met on August 2. The Roman lines pushed forward, but were attacked from the rear by Hannibal's horsemen. The result was a massacre. More than 50,000 Roman soldiers were killed.

BEASTLY PROTECTION

The Carthaginians wore elaborate breastplates and fought with long spears and javelins. They rode elephants in battle, although if panicked, these beasts could flatten their own soldiers. Their Numidian allies from North Africa rode horses without saddles, controlling them with sticks and spoken commands. Celtic allies from France used swords and spears.

THE ROMANS CALLED THE CARTHAGINIANS THE POENI ("PHOENICIANS") AND SO THE THREE WARS BETWEEN THEM BECAME KNOWN AS THE PUNIC WARS.

Third Punic War 149–146 BC

Carthage was heavily defeated in the Second Punic War. However, many Romans still considered Carthage to be a threat. In 149 BC, Rome sent a large army to lay siege to Carthage. The siege went on for three years until starvation and disease weakened resistance. In spring 146 BC, the Romans broke through the city walls. All 50,000 inhabitants surrendered.

▲ When seizing Carthage, the Romans demolished every building and sent its people into slavery

Hilltop SIEGE

High above the Dead Sea in Israel lies the hilltop fortress of Masada. In AD 72, 960 Jewish rebels, who were fighting the Roman occupiers of their country, retreated to this bleak place. The Roman army of 15,000 men laid siege to the fortress for five months. When the Romans finally broke in on April 16, AD 73, they were met with a terrible sight.

THE TARGET—MASADA

The fortress of Masada stood on a rocky hilltop 1,300 ft (400 m) above the Dead Sea. A long wall with many towers surrounded the fortress. Inside were a palace, barracks, armory, and many storehouses. Tanks collected rainwater for drinking. The only access to the fortress was by three narrow paths that led up to fortified gates.

▼ The Masada fortress ruins and surrounding siegeworks are now a UNESCO site.

Northern Palace

Storehouses

Watch Tower

WHEN UNDER ATTACK, GROUPS OF SOLDIERS HELD SHIELDS AROUND THEM TO FORM A TESTUDO (TORTOISE).

BOUDICCA'S REVOLT

The Roman Empire faced many uprisings during its lifetime. Shortly before the Jewish Revolt in AD 73, the Iceni tribe, led by Queen Boudicca, took London and other cities. In a major battle in AD 60, the Romans massacred tens of thousands of Iceni. Boudicca died, probably by taking poison.

▶ A statue of Boudicca and her daughters stands by the river Thames in London, U.K.

At Masada, the ruins of many Roman camps remain, showing stone walls on which soldiers erected their tents.

STEP 3: GET INSIDE THE WALLS

Once inside, the Romans discovered that the Jewish leader, Eleazar Ben Yai'r, had encouraged all of his supporters to commit suicide. Of the 960 defenders, 953 killed themselves. Only two women and five children were found alive, hiding in a drain.

The Roman siege tower was slowly pushed up a ramp on the western side of Masada. Once at the top, it battered its way through the fortress walls.

Western Palace

Place where Romans breached the walls

Western Palace

Siege tower

▼ The ramp was 1,970 ft (600 m) long and rose to a height of more than 600 ft (200 m).

Ramp

Roman camp

Dry riverbed

STEP 2: SMASH THROUGH

The Romans pushed a siege tower up the ramp to break through the walls. At the front of the tower was a battering ram to knock through, and mounted on top were ballistas (catapults) to hurl rocks. Strong wooden walls protected the soldiers inside the tower.

STEP 1: BUILD A RAMP

In late AD 72, the Romans surrounded Masada. They soon realized a blockade—cutting off food, water, and communication—would be too slow as the Jews had plenty of provisions within the walls. The Romans needed to get inside quickly, bypassing the hazardous access paths. The plan was to build a huge ramp up the western side of the hill. The Romans were under constant attack during construction, but they continued until it was complete.

Death from the Sea

From 793 onward, the Anglo-Saxons of England faced a new threat from the sea. Viking invaders swept up to the coast in their longboats, killing and plundering everywhere they landed. The Anglo-Saxon defenders were brave, but the Vikings more cunning, and battles often led to masses of Anglo-Saxon deaths. Although the Anglo-Saxons formed a number of small kingdoms, their warriors were rarely a match for the ferocious Vikings.

▲ The prow of a longboat was carved with a dragon or beast to strike fear into Viking enemies.

Fearsome longships

Viking raiders traveled the seas in wooden longships. These vessels were up to 71 ft (22 m) long and 16 ft (5 m) wide, and carried a crew of up to 30 warriors. The ships had shallow hulls, so they could sail inland up rivers. In a raid, the Vikings could drag the ships onto a beach—and escape quickly afterward!

The Battle of Maldon

In August 991, a Viking invasion fleet sailed to Essex in eastern England, landing on Northey Island. When the tide was out, the Vikings made their way along the causeway to the mainland, but found their passage blocked by an Anglo-Saxon force of 3,000 men. Viking king Olaf Tryggvason asked that his men be allowed to pass and Anglo-Saxon leader Byrhtnoth agreed. Once on land, the Vikings turned on their enemies and killed them all in battle.

Fierce warriors

Viking raiders leapt from their longboats to bring terror to those they attacked. They raided for booty and treasure, but also looked for land to settle on and countries to rule. They valued glory more than life. Before battle, berserker warriors dressed in animal skins and worked themselves up by shouting and biting their shields. They charged at the enemy, howling like wild animals.

▼ Viking cunning won the day at Maldon, tricking the Anglo-Saxons into a battle they could not win.

Slice and slash

The main Viking weapons were axes, swords, and spears, all made of iron. Long, double-edged swords were used to deliver slashing blows rather than for stabbing the enemy. Horsemen thrust long-handled spears through walls of shields. Spears, arrows, and axes were all thrown at an enemy during a battle. Round shields protected the warriors during combat.

▶ Battleaxes had iron blades up to 12 in (30 cm) across and wooden shafts up to 6.5 ft (2 m) long.

Mass Murder

The Mongols were brutal warriors, killing every enemy they met. Winning battle after battle, they eventually carved out a massive empire that stretched from China in the east across Asia to the Black Sea in the west. In 1258, Mongol armies led by Hulagu captured Baghdad. The city was about to be slaughtered.

Genghis Khan was a fearless warrior. By the time of his death in 1227, he ruled the largest empire in history.

The reign of Genghis Khan

The Mongols were nomadic people who lived on the grassy steppes of Mongolia to the north of China. The young Genghis Khan united the warring Mongol tribes and in 1206 was chosen to be their leader. He invaded northern China and soon controlled much of central Asia. His son Ogetai conquered Russia and reached eastern Europe and the Mediterranean Sea.

Mounted warriors

The Mongols were fine horsemen, riding strong horses over great distances. Each warrior had a string of horses and changed mounts often, so as not to tire them. Skilled archers rained down arrows on their enemies, while soldiers armed with long lances engaged in close combat.

Mongol warriors wore leather armor and helmets, and carried small, round leather shields.

THE MONGOL EMPIRE

1206   Genghis Khan unites Mongol tribes under his leadership

1211   Genghis Khan invades northern China

1219   Mongols conquer central Asia

1237   Mongols invade Russia

1241   Mongols invade eastern Europe and defeat major German army in Poland

1258   **Led by Hulagu, the Mongols seize Baghdad**

1259   Mongol Empire breaks into separate states

1268-79   Mongols under Kublai Khan conquer southern China

Taking on Baghdad

In 1256, Hulagu—the grandson of Genghis Khan—led his Mongol forces toward Baghdad. The caliph refused to accept Mongol rule and closed the city's gates. Meanwhile, another Mongol force lured a Muslim division onto marshy ground, breached the dykes of the river Euphrates, and drowned them all.

▲ Hulagu ruled the Mongols from 1256 until his death in 1265. During his reign, his armies captured Baghdad and much of the Middle East.

The deadly siege

Hulagu surrounded Baghdad and in February 1258, the Mongol army broke in. They forced the caliph to surrender and massacred all 90,000 inhabitants. The caliph was spared until he revealed where the treasury was hidden. He was then rolled up in a carpet and trampled to death.

▲ The Mongols besieged the city, and once inside the walls, they burned the buildings to the ground.

129

Although outnumbered, the Minamoto army ambushed the Taira clan and won the Battle of Kurikara.

Sly Samurai

Samurai—the name that brought terror to their enemies. These skilled Japanese warriors fought and died for their masters. Riding into battle on horses, they often dismounted to engage in brutal one-on-one combat, fighting to the death. The winner cut off his opponent's head as proof of his courage and skill.

War at Kurikara

In 1183, a vast Taira army of 100,000 men advanced north to meet the rival Minamoto clan, half its size, at Kurikara. They took up position at the top of a mountain pass and carried out a lengthy archery duel with the Minamoto army in the valley below. While this went on, Minamoto soldiers crept round the enemy's rear and sent a herd of oxen with burning torches tied to their horns up the pass toward the Taira army. The Taira fled in panic, many falling to their deaths from the mountain paths. The rest were massacred. The victorious Minamoto could now take over Japan.

Battle warriors

Samurai were an elite warrior class with a strong code of honor known as *bushido*, which told them how to behave in life. Battle would often start after an argument between rival clans. When the two sides faced each other on a battlefield, the armies followed a strict sequence of events. First, champions from each side rode out to meet each other. The two men would fight on horseback, then take part in hand-to-hand combat. After the duel, fighting broke out between the whole army.

◄ In single combat, samurai fought with swords that had long, curved blades.

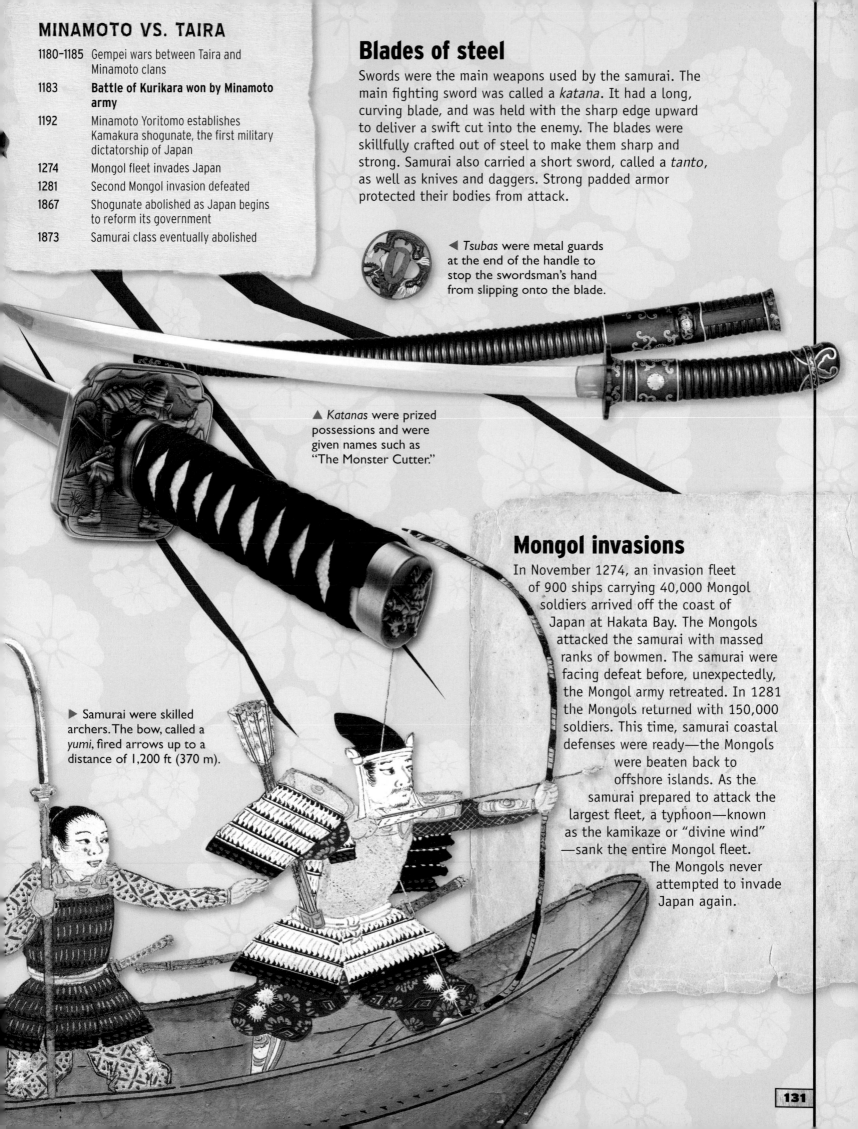

Blades of steel

Swords were the main weapons used by the samurai. The main fighting sword was called a *katana*. It had a long, curving blade, and was held with the sharp edge upward to deliver a swift cut into the enemy. The blades were skillfully crafted out of steel to make them sharp and strong. Samurai also carried a short sword, called a *tanto*, as well as knives and daggers. Strong padded armor protected their bodies from attack.

◄ *Tsubas* were metal guards at the end of the handle to stop the swordsman's hand from slipping onto the blade.

▲ *Katanas* were prized possessions and were given names such as "The Monster Cutter."

► Samurai were skilled archers. The bow, called a *yumi*, fired arrows up to a distance of 1,200 ft (370 m).

Mongol invasions

In November 1274, an invasion fleet of 900 ships carrying 40,000 Mongol soldiers arrived off the coast of Japan at Hakata Bay. The Mongols attacked the samurai with massed ranks of bowmen. The samurai were facing defeat before, unexpectedly, the Mongol army retreated. In 1281 the Mongols returned with 150,000 soldiers. This time, samurai coastal defenses were ready—the Mongols were beaten back to offshore islands. As the samurai prepared to attack the largest fleet, a typhoon—known as the kamikaze or "divine wind" —sank the entire Mongol fleet. The Mongols never attempted to invade Japan again.

100 Years of War

The longest war in history—known as the Hundred Years War—began in 1337 and ended in 1453, a total of 116 years. The war began when the French claimed the throne. After many bloody battles, the English were thrown out of France. When Edward III of England ended the war out of France.

Crécy, 1346

The first major battle of the war took place near Crécy, northern France. The small English army took up position on a slope. When the much larger French army arrived, they were tired and wet after a long march. Facing the sun, the French crossbowmen fired first—but their bolts fell short and they were quickly cut down by English arrows. Next, the French knights charged at the English, but the defense was too strong and the French soldiers fell. At least 4,000 Frenchmen were killed, but only 200 English.

▲ The French used crossbows—deadly but slow to load and fire. The English used longbows—firing 12 arrows a minute with deadly accuracy.

Poitiers, 1356

The second English victory came in 1356 at Poitiers, western France. The English took up position behind a large hedge with a narrow gap through which only four knights could ride abreast. Wave after wave of French knights rode toward the gap, only for their horses to be shot down by the English archers. Finally, the English army charged at the French and attacked them from the rear.

▲ King John II of France surrendered to Edward the Black Prince, commander of the English army, at Poitiers.

Agincourt, 1415

After a long pause, Henry V of England renewed his claim to the French throne and sailed for France. An exhausted 6,000-strong English army faced a French army of 20,000 men. The English planted themselves in woodland by a narrow road. As the French horsemen and foot soldiers became bogged down in muddy ground, the English attacked, clearing the field—another victory. More than 5,000 French soldiers died, with only 300 English deaths.

▲ At the start of the Battle of Agincourt, Henry V of England and his army prayed for victory.

HUNDRED YEARS WAR

1337	Edward III of England claims French throne and declares war
1340	English win naval battle at Sluys
1346	**Victory for English at Crécy**
1347	English seize Calais after long siege
1356	**English win at Poitiers and take French king prisoner**
1360	Peace of Brétigny brings temporary halt to the war, leaving English in control of much of southern France
1369	Fighting resumes as French slowly expel English from France
1415	**Henry V renews his claim to the throne and wins at Agincourt**
1420	Henry V becomes heir to the French throne but dies in 1422
1429	Joan of Arc ends siege of Orléans
1453	War ends with England only in control of Calais, which it holds until 1558

Steel protection

Knights had the best arms and armor and were the most experienced, skilled fighters in an army. Early knights wore chainmail armor, but enemies soon learned how to deliver piercing blows. During the 14th century, plate armor was developed, which was much more difficult for swords and arrows to penetrate. It was made of sheets of steel shaped to fit the body. The helmet was also made of metal, with a hinged visor that could be lifted up and down. A full suit of armor weighed about 55 lb (25 kg).

▼ A suit of armor covered the body, arms, and legs. Although heavy, it was flexible enough for the knight to bend and twist.

AGAINST the Odds

The fall of the Inca Empire to the Spanish in 1532 was extraordinary. Armed with guns and horses, which were both unknown to the Incas, less than 200 Spaniards overwhelmed an army of at least 40,000 men and soon captured an empire of 12 million people.

A GREAT EMPIRE

The Inca Empire stretched down the west coast of South America, from what is now Ecuador in the north to Chile in the south. The Incas were great farmers, building terraces along the steep hillsides to plant crops. They connected their long, thin empire together with 12,500 mi (20,100 km) of roads, the greatest road network built since the Roman Empire 1,000 years before.

SOUTH AMERICA

Capturing the empire

In 1532, a long civil war that weakened the Incan Empire ended. Spanish conquistador Pizarro and his 178 men advanced safely inland. On the morning of November 16, Pizarro met the Incan ruler Atahualpa and his 40,000 men at Cajamarca, Peru. The Spanish opened fire and seized Atahualpa. They ransomed him for a room filled with gold, but later killed him. Pizarro then marched on Cuzco, the capital, which he took without a fight.

▼ The small Spanish army used superior weaponry to overwhelm the Incas. They had steel swords, helmets, and armor, as well as small cannon, compared to unarmed Incan soldiers wearing leather armor.

▲ Pizarro led the expedition through the Andes on the way to Cajamarca. He was a daring commander whose nerve enabled him to capture a vast empire.

PIZARRO'S PLIGHT

Francisco Pizarro was born into poverty in Spain sometime in the early 1470s. He never learned to read or write. He sailed on a couple of expeditions to South America before leading two expeditions to conquer the Inca Empire in 1524 and 1526. Both ended in failure. After he discovered gold and gemstones in northern Peru, he made a third successful attempt in 1532. A quarrel led to his death in 1541.

▼ Despite their defeat in 1532, the Incas continued to resist Spanish rule, rising in rebellion in 1536 and fighting the Spanish until their leader was killed in 1572.

Armed to fight

The Spanish fought the Incas with crossbows, swords, and arquebuses—muskets that used a lit match to ignite the charge that shot the bullet. Above all, they had horses, animals that were unknown to the Incas. In response, the unarmed Incas fought back with stones.

CONQUERING MEXICO

About 11 years before the Spanish overwhelmed the Inca Empire, they had achieved a similar victory over another massive empire thousands of miles to the north. In 1519 Hernán Cortés set out with 600 men and 17 horses to explore the Yucatan Peninsula of Mexico on behalf of the Spanish crown. Within two years he had taken over the mighty Aztec Empire and captured Tenochtitlan, its capital city.

▼ The Aztec capital of Tenochtitlan lay on an island in the middle of the Lake Texcoco in central Mexico.

SPANISH VS. INCAS

1531	Francisco Pizarro lands at Tumbes in Inca Empire and sets off to meet Atahualpa
1532	Civil war ends in Inca Empire with victory for Atahualpa over his brother
Nov 15	Pizarro arrives in Cajamarca
Nov 16	**Pizarro's forces overwhelm the Incas and take Atahualpa hostage**
Jul 26, 1533	After the ransom was paid, Atahualpa is killed by the Spanish
1534	Pizarro enters Cuzco and controls Inca Empire

The Great Fleet

In May 1588, a large invasion fleet was ordered to set sail by Spain's powerful ruler Philip II. The Great Armada was made up of 130 ships fitted with 2,500 guns, and carried 30,000 soldiers and sailors. The ships included large warships called galleons, galleys, and supply vessels. It was headed toward England, sent to overthrow Queen Elizabeth I of England and conquer her country.

Battered ships

The Armada was first spotted off the south coast of England on July 29, 1588. On August 7, eight English ships were set alight and sent into the Spanish fleet, forcing the Spanish to cut their anchor cables and flee. The next day the two sides met off Gravelines, northern France. Five Spanish ships were sunk or captured in an eight-hour battle. The badly damaged Armada was driven northward, scattered by gales. The threat to England was over.

▼ The Spanish Armada sailed in close formation up the English Channel, attacked along the way by English ships.

THE ENEMY QUEEN

Elizabeth I came to the throne of England in 1558 after the death of her sister, Mary I. Mary, a Roman Catholic, had been married to Philip II of Spain. Elizabeth, however, was a Protestant and thus an enemy of Catholic Spain. Elizabeth supported the seadogs who captured Spanish treasure ships and sent support to the Dutch in their fight for independence from Spanish rule. Elizabeth ruled England until her death in 1603.

▲ Elizabeth was crowned queen of England in January 1559. Although much-loved by her people, she never married.

SPANISH VS. ENGLISH

1556	Philip II becomes king of Spain
1558	Elizabeth I becomes queen of England
1585	Elizabeth helps Dutch rebels fight against Spanish rule
1587	Elizabeth executes Mary Queen of Scots, a Catholic rival to her throne
April 29-30	Drake attacks Spanish fleet at Cadiz
May 28, 1588	Armada sets sail toward England
July 29	Armada sighted off the Lizard Peninsula in Cornwall
August 6	Armada anchors off Calais
August 7	England sends eight fireships to break up Spanish fleet
August 8	**Battle of Gravelines**
August 9	Wind drives Armada into North Sea
1598	Philip dies
1603	Elizabeth dies

Shipwreck!

The English pursued the Armada up the North Sea to Scotland, from where it sailed north round the British Isles and down the Atlantic Ocean to Spain. More than 50 ships were shipwrecked by storms on the Scottish and Irish coasts and at least 20,000 men lost their lives. Just 67 ships limped home to Spain.

▼ Small, fast English ships carrying long-range guns chased and defeated the large Spanish galleons.

▲ Francis Drake was knighted by Queen Elizabeth in 1581 on board his ship the *Golden Hind*, which he'd used to voyage round the world.

THE QUEEN'S PIRATE

English sailors, notably Francis Drake, regularly attacked Spanish galleons laden with gold from the New World (the Americas). In April 1587, Drake attacked the port of Cadiz and destroyed much of the Spanish fleet preparing to join the Armada. This delayed the Armada by about a year.

The Siege of
THE ALAMO

The Siege of the Alamo in 1836 did not involve large armies or result in masses of deaths. Only 189 Texan men were besieged by a force of 1,500 Mexican troops. All the defenders lost their lives, but the cause they fought for—the independence of Texas from Mexican rule— was soon achieved.

The stronghold

In 1836, as fighting between Mexico and Texas became more fierce, a group of Texan volunteers drove the Mexicans out of San Antonio, Texas, and occupied the Alamo, an old mission building. They were urged to withdraw by the Texan commander, Sam Houston, as he felt their position was too exposed. They refused.

◀ 1,500 Mexican troops advanced on the Alamo, armed with rifles and muskets.

MEXICANS VS. TEXANS

1740s	Work begins building the Alamo
1830	After U.S. migrants pour into Texas, Mexico closes the Texan–U.S. border
1835	Mexico removes rights enjoyed by Texas. Texas revolts and drives Mexican troops out of the state
Feb 23–Mar 6, 1836	**Siege of the Alamo**
March 2, 1836	Texas declares independence from Mexico
April 21, 1836	Sam Houston defeats Mexicans at San Jacinto
1845	Texas joins the U.S.

THE ALAMO'S HERO

Davy Crockett (1786–1836) is a U.S. folk hero, known to millions as the "King of the Wild Frontier." He was born in rural Tennessee and gained a reputation for storytelling. In 1826 he became a member of the U.S. Congress, but lost his seat in 1834. Fed up with his failure, he went to fight for Texan independence and was one of the men killed at the Alamo.

► Crockett became well known for being a strong frontiersman and soldier—and later in life, a politician.

TO THE DEATH

On February 23, a Mexican force reached San Antonio and besieged the Alamo for 13 days. In the early hours of March 6, they attacked while the Texans were asleep. The Texans soon woke and fired at the advancing enemy, but their fight was hopeless. Within 90 minutes, all 189 defenders lay dead.

▼ As the Texan defenders fired their guns over the walls, new guns were loaded behind them.

DECLARING INDEPENDENCE

While the siege of the Alamo continued, Texas declared its independence from Mexico. In April 1836, Texan commander Sam Houston defeated the Mexican army at San Jacinto. Texas then became an independent republic and remained so until it joined the U.S. in 1845 as the 28th state of the Union.

The LAST STAND

In the 1800s, the U.S. government tried to confine the Sioux to special reservations, but they continued to hunt for buffalo across the Black Hills of Dakota. As American prospectors moved into the area in search of gold, the Sioux felt threatened. On June 25, 1876, they fought back at one of the most famous battles on American soil, the Battle of the Little Bighorn.

The fatal battle

On June 25, 1876, George Custer and 210 men of the 7th Cavalry surveyed the area near the Little Bighorn River, Montana, and spotted Sioux encampments. Disobeying orders, they attacked immediately. Custer came under ferocious attack from 2,500 Sioux, who fired volleys of arrows down on them. Custer ordered his men to kill their horses and use the bodies as a barrier, but it was too late—every cavalryman was killed.

The Sioux

The Lakota and Dakota tribes of Native Americans were known as the Sioux, from the local Chippewa word for "enemy." They lived on the western Great Plains in what are now the states of the Dakotas, Minnesota, and Montana. A warlike people, they were skilled horsemen, firing arrows from their saddles with great accuracy. They carried heavy stone clubs, tomahawks or axes, and scalping knives, as well as shields for protection.

▲ For close combat, the Sioux used warclubs with a metal blade.

Warrior chiefs

Crazy Horse (c. 1840–1877) and Sitting Bull (c. 1831–1890) led their tribes during struggles with the U.S. army and white settlers. They wanted to stop them taking the Sioux land—hunting buffalo was vital to their survival—and this led to a series of battles. Crazy Horse wanted "peace and to be left alone."

◄ Sioux chief Sitting Bull led his people to victory over the U.S. Cavalry at Little Bighorn.

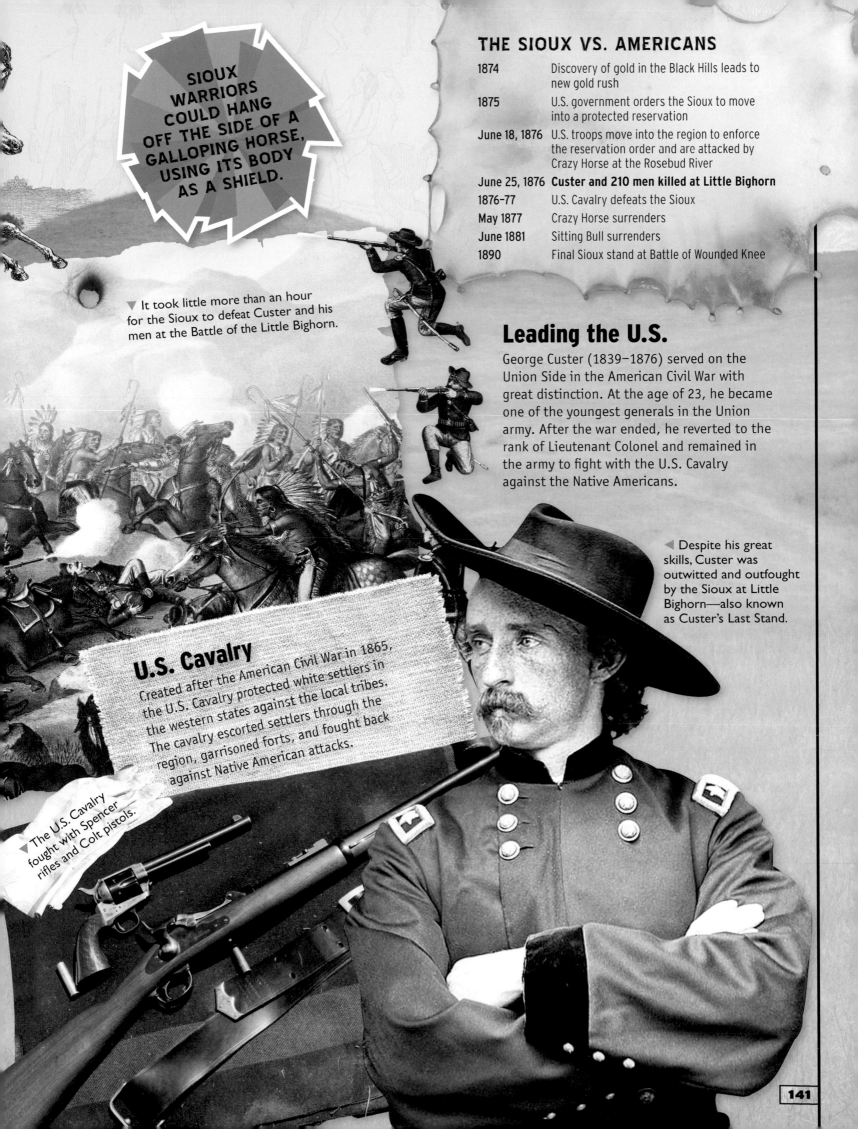

SIOUX WARRIORS COULD HANG OFF THE SIDE OF A GALLOPING HORSE, USING ITS BODY AS A SHIELD.

THE SIOUX VS. AMERICANS

1874	Discovery of gold in the Black Hills leads to new gold rush
1875	U.S. government orders the Sioux to move into a protected reservation
June 18, 1876	U.S. troops move into the region to enforce the reservation order and are attacked by Crazy Horse at the Rosebud River
June 25, 1876	**Custer and 210 men killed at Little Bighorn**
1876-77	U.S. Cavalry defeats the Sioux
May 1877	Crazy Horse surrenders
June 1881	Sitting Bull surrenders
1890	Final Sioux stand at Battle of Wounded Knee

▼ It took little more than an hour for the Sioux to defeat Custer and his men at the Battle of the Little Bighorn.

Leading the U.S.

George Custer (1839–1876) served on the Union Side in the American Civil War with great distinction. At the age of 23, he became one of the youngest generals in the Union army. After the war ended, he reverted to the rank of Lieutenant Colonel and remained in the army to fight with the U.S. Cavalry against the Native Americans.

◀ Despite his great skills, Custer was outwitted and outfought by the Sioux at Little Bighorn—also known as Custer's Last Stand.

U.S. Cavalry

Created after the American Civil War in 1865, the U.S. Cavalry protected white settlers in the western states against the local tribes. The cavalry escorted settlers through the region, garrisoned forts, and fought back against Native American attacks.

▼ The U.S. Cavalry fought with Spencer rifles and Colt pistols.

ZULU Power

As the British expanded their empire across southern Africa, they came into contact with the Zulus —skilled warriors whose bravery and discipline more than made up for their lack of modern weapons. In 1879 the two sides went to war.

Poorly armed, the British troops were overwhelmed by strong Zulu forces.

Major defeat

In January 1879, a British army led by Lord Chelmsford invaded the Zulu kingdom. Chelmsford divided his army in two, leaving 800 British troops and 1,000 African colonial troops camped at Isandhlwana. On January 22, 20,000 Zulus attacked the camp. The slaughter was huge—more than 1,300 British and colonial troops lost their lives. The Zulus lost about 1,000 men. It was one of the worst defeats ever suffered by the British army.

British troops wore striking red uniforms and carried rifles and bayonets.

British forces

The British army consisted of volunteer troops who normally served for four to eight years, with a maximum length of service of 21 years. Soldiers were paid a daily wage and were required to have a basic level of education.

Barefoot warriors

At 18 years old, Zulu boys became warriors. They fought each other in mock battles and went on forced marches and military maneuvers. In battle, they fought barefoot, throwing spears at the enemy and then attacking at close range with wooden clubs and short, stabbing spears. They never took prisoners, killing their opponents and opening their bodies to release the spirits.

◀ Zulu warriors used their shields as offensive weapons to throw their opponents off balance.

▼ A small British force heroically defended Rorke's Drift against a far larger Zulu army.

Rorke's Drift

On the evening of the main battle, 140 British troops, who were defending a nearby river crossing at Rorke's Drift, came under attack from 4,000 Zulus. The British quickly erected a barricade of wagons and grain bags and fought off the Zulus, using long bayonets against Zulu spears. The Zulus attacked all night but eventually withdrew in the morning. Only 17 British troops and 350 Zulus lost their lives. Eleven Victoria Crosses—the highest medal for valor—were awarded to the British soldiers.

BRITISH VS. ZULUS

1816	Paramount chief Shaka rules the Zulus and creates an army
Dec 1878	British issue ultimatum to Zulu king Cetshwayo requiring him to accept British rule
Jan 22–23, 1879	**British invade, but are defeated by Zulus at Isandhlwana. British hold off Zulus at Rorke's Drift**
March 1879	British suffer further defeats
July 4, 1879	Heavily reinforced British army defeats Zulus at Ulundi and ends Zulu independence

OVER the Top

The Battle of the Somme has gone down in history as one of the bloodiest battles ever. In 1916 the British army planned to knock a large hole in the German front line near the river Somme, northern France. However, on the first day of the battle—July 1—the British suffered a catastrophic defeat.

Smashing the lines

On June 26, the British used massive artillery pieces to pound the enemy's defenses, but many of the shells did not explode. The British gunners did not realize that the Germans had rebuilt their defenses using concrete, which wasn't damaged by light shells.

Trench warfare

When the bombardment stopped on July 1, the Germans emerged from their safe dugouts deep underground to man the trenches and machine guns. The British troops advanced, expecting the Germans to have been killed. The soldiers were mown down by German gunfire— 622 men were lost in only 10 minutes. On the first day, 57,470 British troops were killed or injured. By the time the battle ended in November, more than 1.2 million men had been killed or wounded on both sides. Neither side had gained any advantage.

A British 8-in howitzer fired a 200 lb (91 kg) shell a distance of up to 31,500 ft (9,600 m).

BRITISH ARMY

At the start of the war, the British army consisted largely of volunteers who had signed up to fight the Germans. In 1916 they were joined by conscripts—men forced into the army. The standard weapon was the Lee-Enfield rifle, with a bayonet on the end. Soldiers used grenades and mortars against enemy trenches.

Both armies dug themselves into deep, defensive trenches along the Western Front. Firing steps were built so soldiers could aim their rifles over the top without being too exposed.

IN JUNE 1917 THE BRITISH INSTALLED ONE MILLION LB (453,600 KG) OF EXPLOSIVES UNDER GERMAN LINES AT MESSINES. THE EXPLOSION KILLED 10,000 GERMANS AND WAS SO LOUD, IT WAS HEARD 130 MI (210 KM) AWAY IN LONDON.

▲ Soldiers kept their heads down when firing machine guns, as fire was immediately returned by the enemy.

GERMAN ARMY

Every German male, aged 17–45, took part in military service during peacetime. During the war, these conscripts became highly disciplined, effective troops. They were better educated and trained than their enemies. The Germans were the first to dig trenches, which they even equipped with electricity and piped water.

Deadly shot

Both sides used machine guns to deadly effect. These guns, such as the British Vickers and French Hotchkiss, were mounted on tripods and could fire up to 450 bullets a minute. Lighter, more portable machine guns were also used.

CENTRAL POWERS VS. ALLIES

Aug 1914   War breaks out in Europe as Germany invades Belgium and France. Germany, Austria-Hungary, and Turkey (Central Powers) fight Britain, France, and Russia (Allies)

Sept 1914   German advance into France halted at the river Marne

April 1915 Major battle fought at Ypres, Belgium

Feb 1916   Germans begin massive assault against French town of Verdun

July 1916   **Battle of the Somme**

Sept 1916   British first use tanks in battle

April 1917 U.S. joins war, alongside Britain and France

July 1917   Battle takes place at Passchendaele

March 1918 German advance into France

July 1918   German advance reversed

11 Nov 1918 Germans and Allies agree an Armistice to stop fighting, ending the war

SNIPER FIRE

The battle for Stalingrad in southern Russia marked a turning point in World War II. Until then, the Germans had defeated all before them. Now they faced a Soviet enemy determined to hold onto the city at all costs. The battle lasted for six months, with massive loss of life and a major defeat for the Germans.

On June 22, 1941—a year before Stalingrad—Germany invaded the Soviet Union, with an army of more than 3 million men, 3,000 tanks, and 2,500 aircraft. The Soviets were caught by surprise, and within days, their air force had been destroyed and 600,000 troops killed or captured.

THE BATTLE OF STALINGRAD

In August 1942, 270,000 German troops attacked the city of Stalingrad. They pushed the Soviet defenders back to a narrow strip of buildings along the west bank of the Volga River. In November, the Soviets responded by surrounding the German forces. After heavy fighting, the Germans surrendered in February 1943. Around 750,000 German troops were killed or injured. The Soviets lost 1.1 million men.

▶ Thousands of Soviet troops were captured by the Germans as they advanced toward Stalingrad.

▶ Soviet troops threw grenades at German soldiers who were sheltering in the buildings of Stalingrad.

GERMANS VS. SOVIETS

Jun 22, 1941 Germany and its allies invade the Soviet Union
Sep 15, 1941 900-day siege of Leningrad (modern-day St. Petersburg) by Germans
Nov 23, 1941 Germans within reach of Moscow
Aug 19, 1942 **Attack on Stalingrad by German forces**
Nov 23, 1942 Soviet army surrounds German army at Stalingrad
Feb 2, 1943 Germans surrender at Stalingrad

THE SNIPERS

In the ruined buildings of Stalingrad, trained snipers from both sides picked off enemy soldiers one by one. The snipers even fought each other from different floors of the same building. Soviet snipers who killed 40 Germans received bravery medals and the title of "noble sniper."

▼ A rifle's telescopic sight magnifies the sniper's target.

▼ Up to 4,000 Soviet tanks took part in the battle to lift the German siege of Stalingrad.

THE CITY IN RUINS

Named after the Soviet leader, Josef Stalin, the industrial city of Stalingrad lay on the Volga River in southern Russia. The Germans were determined to capture the city named after their main enemy, while the Soviets had to defend the honor of their leader. The battle reduced the city to ruins. Every building was destroyed or seriously damaged, yet many people continued to live among the ruins. Today the city has been rebuilt, and is known as Volgograd.

▶ German soldiers patrol the ruins of Stalingrad in October 1942.

TANK Attack

In July 1943, a major tank battle took place near the Russian city of Kursk. The Soviet army with 5,000 tanks pushed back the massive German attack of 2,900 tanks. After this victory, the Germans were driven out of the Soviet Union, until their eventual defeat in May 1945.

The Battle of Kursk

In July 1943, the front line between the German and Soviet armies ran in a "bulge" round Kursk, southern Russia. The Germans wanted to capture this bulge, but the Soviets reinforced their troops and dug massive fortifications. On July 5, the Germans attacked with 2,900 tanks and 780,000 men. In response, the Soviets had 1.4 million men and more than 5,000 tanks. The battle was so intense that the tanks often rammed each other off the battlefield.

GERMAN PANZER TANKS

At first, German tanks were superior to any enemy tank, but the sheer numbers and firepower of the Soviet T-34s eventually overwhelmed them. About 9,000 Panzer IVs were produced throughout the war.

▼ Fast and reliable, the Panzer IV was originally built as a support vehicle. It carried five crew into battle.

▼ A line of Soviet T-34 tanks advanced toward the front line. Sturmovik fighters in the sky destroyed any stranded German forces.

▼ At the Battle of Kursk, more than 700 tanks were destroyed in just one day.

The Red Army

In the first months of the war against Germany, the Soviet army were badly led and poorly equipped. They lost millions of men who were either killed or taken prisoner. As the war went on, the Soviets learned how to fight with tanks, achieving great victories against the retreating German army.

▼ Red Army troops gathered to receive instructions from their commander.

SOVIET T-34 TANKS

The T-34 was a four-man tank—rugged, highly mobile and well protected by its armor. Designed to be mechanically simple and easy to produce, it was equipped with a tank gun and two machine guns. The first T-34 rolled off the production line in 1941. By May 1944, the Soviets were producing 1,200 T-34s every month.

INDEX

The Incas built a mountaintop city called Machu Picchu, high in the Andes Mountains, with gardens, a temple, and a fortress. The city was built from large, interlocking stones and watered by a spring at the top of the mountain.

INDEX

Entries in **bold** refer to main subject entries; entries in *italics* refer to illustrations.

ACKNOWLEDGMENTS

The publishers would like to thank the following sources for the use of their photographs:

KEY
A/AL=Alamy, B=Bridgeman, CO=Corbis, D=Dreamstime, F=Fotolia, FLPA=Frank Lane Picture Agency, GI=Getty Images, GW=Glow Images, IS=istockphoto.com, MP=Minden Pictures, N=Newscom, NG=National Geographic Creative, NPL=Nature Picture Library, P=Photoshot, PL=Photolibrary, R=Reuters, RF=Rex Features, S=Shutterstock, SJC=Stuart Jackson-Carter, SPL=Science Photo Library, SS=Superstock, TF=Topfoto

t=top, a=above, b=bottom/below, c=center, l=left, r=right, f=far, m=main, bg=background

FRONT COVER Simon Plant/Corbis, SPINE Kamira/S, BACK COVER Moreno Soppelsa/S, Mikhail Zahranichny/S, Hung Chung Chih/S, Fer Gregory/S, bikeriderlondon/S, PRELIMS 1 lrafael/S, 2–3 V. Kuntsman/S, 4 WitR/S, rodho/S, 5 David H.Seymour/S, St. Nick/S

EXTREME HISTORY 6–7 Warner Bros. Pictures/Helena Productions/ Latina Pictures/Radiant Productions/Plan B Entertainment/MSC 8–9(bg) Jenny Solomon/F, (bg, bl) Binkski/S 8(bl) 2003 Charles Walker/TopFoto, (br) Sandro Vannini/Corbis 9(bl) The Granger Collection/TopFoto, (bc) The Granger Collection/TopFoto, (br) Studio 37/S 10–11(frame) Ladyann/S 10(m) Time & Life Pictures/GI, (tl) grivet/S, (tr) kanate/S 11(c) 2001 Topham/PA/ TopFoto, (cl) Roger-Viollet/TopFoto, (bl) GI 14–15(bg) Hywit Dimyadi/S, (game board) Katherine Welles/S, (map) ilolab/S, (counters) Lars Kastilan/S, (dice) Bombaert Patrick/S, (panels) Stephen Aaron Rees/S 14(heading paper) Jakub Krechowicz/S, (tr) Charles Walker/TopFoto, (cl) Bettmann/Corbis, (bl) National Geographic/GI 15(tl) Bettmann/Corbis, (tr) GI, (bl) GI, (br) Popperfoto/GI 16–17(bg) pashabo/S, (postcard) ronstik/S, (stamps) vesves/S, (colored pins) oriori/S 16(tr) Patryk Kosmider/S, (bl) 2005 TopFoto, (br) Historical Picture Archive/ Corbis 17(tl) Michael Nicholson/Corbis, (tr) Print Collector/HIP/ TopFoto, (bl) The Granger Collection/TopFoto, (br) De Agostini/GI 18–19(t,l–r) ClassicStock/TopFoto, Luisa Ricciarini/TopFoto, Corbis, ullsteinbild/TopFoto, 2002 Topham/UPP/TopFoto, (b, l–r) GI, Bettmann/Corbis, Stapleton/ HIP/TopFoto, RIA Novosti/TopFoto, Topham Picturepoint/TopFoto 20–1(bg) Cindi L/S 20(t) O.V.D./S 21(tr) National Geographic/GI 22–3(bg) Eky Studio/S, (book) charles taylor/S, (blood) robybret/S, (panels) Christopher Hudson/iS 22(l) Bettmann/Corbis, (tr) The Granger Collection/TopFoto, (br) Print Collector/HIP/TopFoto 23(tl) The Granger Collection/TopFoto, (tr) Ullstein Bild/TopFoto, (bl) TopFoto, (br) AFP/GI 24(cl) Maslov Dmitry/S, (cr) Bettmann/ Corbis, (bl) Bettmann/Corbis, (br) Anna Hoychuk/S 25(tl) KUCO/S, (tr) Charles Walker/TopFoto, (bl) World History Archive/TopFoto, (br) Topham/ AP/TopFoto 26–7(blood) Steve Collender/S, (fire) Sergey Mironov/S 26(tr) SuperStock/GI, (b) GI 27(t, bg) JeremyRichards/S, (t) Historical Picture Archive/ Corbis, (bl) TopFoto 28–9(bg) zhanna ocheret/S, (book) Evgenia Sh./S 28(tl) optimarc/S, (cl) GI, (cr) Mary Evans Picture Library/

Alamy, (bl) Studio DMM Photography, Designs & Art/S, (br) ullsteinbild/TopFoto 29(tl) The Granger Collection/ TopFoto, (tr) GI, (tr, fan) Margo Harrison/S, (bl) PoodlesRock/Corbis, (br) GI 30–1(bg) val lawless/S, (bg, stains) Picsfive/S, (c) Bochkarev Photography/S 30(header panel) Sibear/S, (tr, sock) Antonov Roman/S, (tr, bowl) Ron Zmiri/S, (blue napkins) Arogant/S, (white napkins) Lim Yong Hian/S, (folded napkins) Tobik/S, (knife and spoon) Natalia Klenova/S, (wooden spoon) Nekrasov Andrey/S 31(tl, plate) Kulish Viktoriia/S, (tl, mouse) marina ljubanovic/S, (tl, sugar mouse) Lucie Lang/S, (tr, ostrich) Timo Jaakonaho/RF, (tr, camel) mmattner/S, (tr, kebab) S, (c) Martina I. Meyer/S, (cr, glass) jesterlsv/S, (cr, tankard) Peter Lorimer/S, (cr, mug) Lipowski Milan/S, (bl) Sergey Shcherbakoff/S, (bc) Lagui/S, (br) discpicture/S 32–3(bg) L.Watcharapol/S 32(tl) Vitaly Korovin/S, (tl, chain text) Steve Collender/S, (tr) Chyrko Olena/S, (l) Picsfive/S, (cr) Gianni Dagli Orti/Corbis, (bl) The Gallery Collection/Corbis, (br) pandapaw/S, (br, panel) Vitaly Korovin/S 33(tl) David Burrows/S, (tl, window) Lusoimages/S, (tc) GI, (tc, panel) Matthias Pahl/S, (tr, noose) Iwona Grodzka/S, (tr, ear) Washington Post/GI, (cl) M.E. Mulder/S, (cr) Charles Walker/ TopFoto, (bl) William Attard McCarthy/S, (br) S 34–5(bg) charles taylor/S, (nails) dusan964/S, (tags) val lawless/S 34(tr, candle) Litvinenko Anastasia/S, (tr, teeth) Le Do/S, (cr, hot cups) Mary Evans Picture Library/Alamy, (cr, books) Brocreative/S, (bl) Roger-Viollet/RF, (bc) SPbPhoto/S, (br, bottle) Lakhesis/S, (br, cups) Coprid/S 35(tl) The Granger Collection/TopFoto, (tl, leeches) Mircea Bezergheanu/S, (tc) Steve Lovegrove/S, (tr) Classic Image/ Alamy, (r) terekhov igor/S, (cl, bottles) Milos Luzanin/S, (cl, mortar and pestle) Pshenichka/S, (cl, spices) Noraluca/S, (cr) eduard ionescu/S, (bl) Noam Armonn/S, (br) Mary Evans Picture Library/Alamy, (br, bg) F 36–7(t, bg) Rémi Cauzid/S, (b, bg) zhu difeng/S, (mud) Ultrashock/S, (tl, panel) photocell/S, (cl, panel) Excellent backgrounds Here/S, (t, l–r) GI, Fotomas/ TopFoto, Museum of London/HIP/ TopFoto, (b, l–r) Hank Frentz/S, Popperfoto/GI, Corbis 36(br, frame) kak2s/S 37(b, frame) SuriyaPhoto/S 38–9(bg) jayfish/S, (panels) Hintau Aliaksei/S 38(header panel) Raia/S, (t) irin-k/S, (c) Ewa Walicka/S, (bl, sacks) Dee Golden, (bl, glasses) Saveliev Alexey Alexsandrovich/S, (bc) Dreamworks/Everett/RF 39(tl) The Gallery Collection/Corbis, (tr, mud) Ultrashock/S, (tr, helmet) bocky/S, (cl) Mettus/S, (cr) TopFoto, (bc) Leigh Prather/S, (br) AP/ Topham, (br, bg) Ana de Sousa/S 40–1(panels) Dim Dimich/S, (scrolls) koya979/S 40(header panel) inxti/S, (bg) Kompaniets Taras/S, (tr) The Granger Collection/TopFoto (bl) Andrey Burmakin/S 41(tl) Sophy R./S, (tr) papa/S, (tc, silkworms) holbox/S, (tc, scroll) Roman Sigaev/S, (tc, gun) Kellis/S, (c) PaulPaladin/S, (cr) Bettmann/Corbis, (bl) composite image: StudioSmart/S, PhotoHouse/S, (br) Molodec/S

UNEARTH HISTORY 42–3 Mark Campbell/RF; 44–5 Lanica Klein/GI, val lawless/S, (b) Eddie Keogh/Reuters/CO; 44(cl) GI, (tl) Sergey Kamshylin/S, (tr) Sipa Press/RF; 45(br) Kirsanov/S, (c) Nils Jorgensen/RF, (c) Hintau Aliaksei/S, (c) Leigh Prather/S, (tr) West Semitic Research/Dead Sea Scrolls Foundation/CO;

46–7 mack2happy/S, sniegirova mariia/S, (bc) Eastimages/S; 46(bl) Selyutina Olga/S, (br) Jon Bower London/AL, (cl) Cameramannz/S, (cl) Valentin Agapov/S, (cr) GI, (l) Ultrashock/S, (tl) nulinukas/S; 47(br) GI, (c) val lawless/S, (cl) GI, (tr) Brian Rasic/RF, (tr) BW Folsom/S; 48–9 Cristina Ciochina/S, (bc) gary yim/S, (tc) St. Nick's/S; 48(bl) Manda Nicholls/S, (bl) ChaosMaker/S, (cl) Amenhotepov/S; 49(b) Phase4Photography/S, (c) Igor Plotnikov/S, (cr) Yuri Yavnik/S, (r) SeanPavonePhoto/S, (tr) 100ker/S; 50–1 Ed Lemery/S; 50(bl) Werner Forman/CO, (t) Eky Studio/S, (tc) John Lock/S, (tl) Wuttichok/S; 51(r) mrfotos/S, (bl) Time & Life Pictures/GI, (cr) Keren Su/China Span/AL, (tr) Joel Blit/S; 52–3(t) Mary Evans Picture Library/AL; 52(bc) Kapu/S, (bc) Hintau Aliaksei/S, (bl) Pokaz/S, (cr) grintan/S, (r) Dea Picture Library/GI, (tl) Mark Carrel/S; 53(bc) The Art Gallery Collection/AL, (bl) Jill Battaglia/S, (bl) Valentin Agapov/S, (br) Jakub Krechowicz/S, (cl) Sergey Peterman/S, (r) Gianni Dagli Orti/CO, (tl) Leigh Prather/S, (tr) Charles & Josette Lenars/CO, (tr) Valentin Agapov/S, (tr) Kenneth V. Pilon/S; 54–5 Mark Yarchoan/S, (t) De Agostini/GI; 54(br) Kenneth Garrett/National Geographic Stock/GI, (br) Hefr/S, (tl) Anan Kaewkhammul/S, (tl) Anan Kaewkhammul/S; 55(bl) Nattika/S, (br) Jonathan Blair/CO, (c) Anan Kaewkhammul/S, (cl) Spectrum Colour Library/HIP/TF, (cr) Ulza/S, (t) TF; 56–7 Pavol Kmeto/S, (b) Jarno Gonzalez Zarraonandia/S; 56(bl) David Davis/S, (cl) Sergej Razvodovskij/S, (t) Steve Collender/S, (tl) HGalina/S, (tl) Danny Smythe/S, (tl) Khoroshunova Olga/S; 57(b) Nathan Benn/AL, (br) rodho/S, (cr) vittorio sciosia/AL, (tr) nito/S; 58–9 avian/S, (t) Time & Life Pictures/GI; 58(bl) Toni Dal Lago/S, (bl) Dja65/S, (bl) Yuri Shirokov/S, (br) Artem Mazunov/S, (br) niederhaus.g/S, (cl) Holly Kuchera/S, (tl) liubomir/S, (tl) TF, (tr) Werner Forman/CO, (tr) Evgeny Murtola/S; 59(r) Dorling Kindersley/GI, (bc) prism68/S, (bl) Luisa Ricciarini/TF, (c) Werner Forman/CO, (cl) Kamira/S, (cl) Kamira/S, (t) The Granger Collection/TF, (tc) Persian School/GI; 60–1 thepiwko/S, (b) Asian Art & Archaeology, Inc./CO; 60(b) Lucy Baldwin/S, (bc) silky/S, (cr) Paul D Stewart/SPL, (tr) Traci Law/S; 61(cr) altrendo travel/GI, (l) CO, (tr) Eugene Sergeev/S, (tr) italianestro/S; 62–3 Julio Donoso/Sygma/CO; 62(bl) The Granger Collection/TF, (tr) AFP/GI; 63(bl) Copper Age/GI, (br) blinow61/S, (br) Patrick Landmann/SPL, (cr) for you design/S, (tr) TF, (bl) ivn3da/S; 64(bl) James King-Holmes/SPL, (c) WpN/PS, (tl) J. Helgason/S; 65(bl) martiin fluidworkshop/S, (bl) Alexander Tsiaras/SPL, (br) ullsteinbild/TF, (cl) R-studio/S, (tr) Michael Maloney/San Francisco Chronicle/CO, (tr) Linali/S; 66–7 nav/S; 66(b) R-studio/S, (bl) Mimmo Jodice/CO, (cr) Giraudon/B, (l) Vladislav Gurfinkel/S, (tl) Kompaniets Taras/S, (tl) Neo Edmund/S, (tr) Nathan Benn/AL; 67(br) Sergios/S, (l) zhu difeng/S, (t) idea for life/S, (tr) bilwissedition Ltd. & Co. KG/AL; 68–9 Ladyann/S, (t) Classic Image/AL; 68 Bettmann/CO, (c) Lou Oates/S, (b) Jakub Krechowicz/S, (bc) Mike Hollist/Daily Mail/RF, (bl) Richard Cano/IS, (cl) frescomovie/S; 69(b) Brian Harris/RF, (cl) Brian Harris/RF, (tr) GI; 70–1 Borut Furlan/PL, fuyu liu/S; 70(bl) Ancient Art & Architecture Collection Ltd/AL, (cl) Emory Kristof/National Geographic Stock/GI; 71(br) Richard T. Nowitz/CO, (br) Steve Collender/S, (t) Nils Jorgensen/RF; 72–3 Flyfoto/AL, agap/S; 72(bl) Last Refuge/Robert Harding World Imagery/CO; 73(br) Mark Burnett/AL, (tr) Maria Toutoudaki/IS, (tr) Tomas Kunzt/S; 74 Anelina/S, (cl) V. Kuntsman/S, (bl) Phil Yeomans/RF, (bl) Iaroslav Neliubov/S, (br) pzAxe/S, (br) Laborant/S, (tl) Excellent backgrounds/S, (tr) Gamma-Rapho/GI; 75(bl) AFP/GI, (br) Paul Vinten/S, (cr) topal/S, (t) Charles Taylor/S, (tl) ullsteinbild/TF, (tr) Nata Sdobnikova/S; 76–7 pio3/S, (t) B Christopher/AL; 76(br) PA Photos/TF, (cl) imagelab/GI, (cl) Shevchenko Nataliya/S, (t) Ampirion/S; 77(b) Spectrum/HIP/TF, (bl) All Canada Photos/AL, (br) Illman/S, (tr) Jean-Pierre Lescourret/CO

BUILDING HISTORY 78–9 Image Broker/RF, 80–1 Pecold/S, 80(cl) Pictorial Press Ltd/A, 81 (c) Pecold/S, 81(b) The Art Archive/A, 81(t) Government of Ireland National Monuments Service Photographic Unit, 82–3 Henning Dalhoff/SPL, 82–3(t) Nickolay Vinokurov/S, 82(bl) Basileus/S, 82(border) Dmitry Khrustalev/S, 83(br) MICHAEL POLIZA/NG, 83(cl) KENNETH GARRETT/NG, 83(tr) WhiteHaven/S, 84–5(c) Timothy W. Stone/S, 84–5(bed bg) K. Miri Photography/S, 84–5(suitcase bg) 54613/S, 84(bl) Evgeny Karandaev/S, 84(book) Erik Svoboda/S, 84(br) kropic1/S, 84(c) Federico Rostagno/S, 84(cl) Rolf Hicker/All Canada Photos/CO, 84(logo) Milos Dizajn/S, 84(tickets) brandonht/S, 85(c) jason cox/S, 85(bl) S.Borisov/S, 85(br) Lukas Hlavac/S, 85(cl) Roman Gorielov/S, 85(tl) Noppasin/S, 85(towel bg) K. Miri Photography/S, 85(tr) ZRyzner/S, 86–7 Vitalii Nesterchuk/S, 86–7(top bg) Transia Design/S, 86(ct) duncan1890/istockphoto.com, 86(t) Hemis/A, 86(t) Azat1976/S, 87(tl) M. De Ganck/F1online/GW, 87(tr) Design Pics/CO, 88–9(bg) Lucy Baldwin/S, 88(b panel) ARCHITECTEUR/S, 88(cl) aslysun/S, 88(tc) koosen/S, 88(tr) hxdbzxy/S, 89(b main) fotohunter/S, 89(bg panel) Rafa Irusta/Fotolia.com, 89(bg) Konstantin Sutyagin/Fotolia.com, 89(bl main) British Library/The Art Archive, 89(tl) Hsien-Min Yang/NGS Image Collection/The Art Archive, 90–1(main) Bertl123/S, 90(bl) J.S. Johnston/CO, 90(br) Jenny Kennard/Image Source/CO, 90(cl) Rostislav Glinsky/S, 90(cr) Stapleton Collection/CO, 91(b) StevanZZ/S, 91(br paper) David M. Schrader/S, 91(br sign) Picsfive/S, 91(br) xpixel/S, 91(c) JILL SCHNEIDER/NG, 92–3(blue bg) Lizard/fotolia.com, 92(b) CLAUS LUNAU/SPL, 92(bl) Lagui/S, 92(l) tanatat/S, 92(nails) xpixel/S, 92(paper) TADDEUS/S, 92(t) italianestro/S, 93(bl) Heritage Images/CO, 93(br) Brendan Howard/S, 93(tc) Private Collection/Gianni Dagli Orti /The Art Archive, 94–5(blue bg) Lizard/fotolia.com, 94–5(border) Orhan Cam/S, 94–5(gold bg) R-studio/S, 94–5(main) Jose Fuste Raga/GW, 94(bl) The Art Archive/A, 94(tr) travelstock44/LOOK-foto/GW, 95(bl) Historical Picture Archive/CO, 96–7(main) Image Broker/RF, 96–7(panel bgs) Kompaniets Taras/S, 96(bl) National Geographic Image Collection/A, 96(t) elic/S, 97(bl) Ralf Broskvar/S, 97(br) kccullenPhoto/S, 97(cl) steve estvanik/S, 97(cr) Yu Lan/S, 97(tr) National Geographic Image Collection/A, 98–9(main) Michele Falzone/JAI/CO, 98(b) Madlen/S, 98(bl) Luca Tettoni/CO, 98(bl) nito/S, 98(border) SignStudio/S, 98(br) Luca I. Tettoni/CO,